Crime (Sentences) Act 1997

CHAPTER 43

ARRANGEMENT OF SECTIONS

Crime (Sentences) Act 1997

1997 CHAPTER 43

An Act to make further provision with respect to the treatment of offenders; and for connected purposes.   [21st March 1997]

B E IT ENACTED by the Queen's most Excellent Majesty, by and with the advice and consent of the Lords Spiritual and Temporal, and Commons, in this present Parliament assembled, and by the authority of the same, as follows:—

PART I

MANDATORY AND MINIMUM CUSTODIAL SENTENCES

1.—(1) This section has effect for the purposes of setting out the basis on which the court shall carry out its sentencing functions under this Part.

(2) Under section 2 below, when determining whether it would be appropriate not to impose a life sentence the court shall have regard to the circumstances relating to either of the offences or to the offender.

(3) Under sections 3 and 4 below, when determining whether it would be appropriate not to impose a custodial sentence of at least seven years under section 3(2) or, as the case may be, of at least three years under section 4(2) the court shall have regard to the specific circumstances which—

    (a) relate to any of the offences or to the offender; and

    (b) would make the prescribed custodial sentence unjust in all the circumstances.

Conditions relating to mandatory and minimum custodial sentences.

2.—(1) This section applies where—

    (a) a person is convicted of a serious offence committed after the commencement of this section; and

    (b) at the time when that offence was committed, he was 18 or over and had been convicted in any part of the United Kingdom of another serious offence.

(2) The court shall impose a life sentence, that is to say—

Mandatory life sentence for second serious offence.

(a) where the person is 21 or over, a sentence of imprisonment for life;

(b) where he is under 21, a sentence of custody for life under section 8(2) of the Criminal Justice Act 1982 ("the 1982 Act"),

1982 c.48.

unless the court is of the opinion that there are exceptional circumstances relating to either of the offences or to the offender which justify its not doing so.

(3) Where the court does not impose a life sentence, it shall state in open court that it is of that opinion and what the exceptional circumstances are.

(4) An offence the sentence for which is imposed under subsection (2) above shall not be regarded as an offence the sentence for which is fixed by law.

(5) An offence committed in England and Wales is a serious offence for the purposes of this section if it is any of the following, namely—

(a) an attempt to commit murder, a conspiracy to commit murder or an incitement to murder;

1861 c.100.

(b) an offence under section 4 of the Offences Against the Person Act 1861 (soliciting murder);

(c) manslaughter;

(d) an offence under section 18 of the Offences Against the Person Act 1861 (wounding, or causing grievous bodily harm, with intent);

(e) rape or an attempt to commit rape;

1956 c.69.

(f) an offence under section 5 of the Sexual Offences Act 1956 (intercourse with a girl under 13);

(g) an offence under section 16 (possession of a firearm with intent to injure), section 17 (use of a firearm to resist arrest) or section 18 (carrying a firearm with criminal intent) of the Firearms Act 1968; and

1968 c.27.

(h) robbery where, at some time during the commission of the offence, the offender had in his possession a firearm or imitation firearm within the meaning of that Act.

(6) An offence committed in Scotland is a serious offence for the purposes of this section if the conviction for it was obtained on indictment in the High Court of Justiciary and it is any of the following, namely—

(a) culpable homicide;

(b) attempted murder, incitement to commit murder or conspiracy to commit murder;

(c) rape or attempted rape;

(d) clandestine injury to women or an attempt to cause such injury;

(e) sodomy, or an attempt to commit sodomy, where the complainer, that is to say, the person against whom the offence was committed, did not consent;

(f) assault where the assault—

(i) is aggravated because it was carried out to the victim's severe injury or the danger of the victim's life; or

(ii) was carried out with an intention to rape or to ravish the victim;

(g) robbery where, at some time during the commission of the offence, the offender had in his possession a firearm or imitation firearm within the meaning of the Firearms Act 1968;

1968 c.27.

(h) an offence under section 16 (possession of a firearm with intent to injure), section 17 (use of a firearm to resist arrest) or section 18 (carrying a firearm with criminal intent) of that Act;

(i) lewd, libidinous or indecent behaviour or practices; and

(j) an offence under section 5(1) of the Criminal Law (Consolidation) (Scotland) Act 1995 (unlawful intercourse with a girl under 13).

1995 c.39.

(7) An offence committed in Northern Ireland is a serious offence for the purposes of this section if it is any of the following, namely—

(a) an offence falling within any of paragraphs (a) to (e) of subsection (5) above;

(b) an offence under section 4 of the Criminal Law Amendment Act 1885 (intercourse with a girl under 14);

1885 c.69.

(c) an offence under Article 17 (possession of a firearm with intent to injure), Article 18(1) (use of a firearm to resist arrest) or Article 19 (carrying a firearm with criminal intent) of the Firearms (Northern Ireland) Order 1981; and

S.I. 1981/155 (N.I.2).

(d) robbery where, at some time during the commission of the offence, the offender had in his possession a firearm or imitation firearm within the meaning of that Order.

3.—(1) This section applies where—

Minimum of seven years for third class A drug trafficking offence.

(a) a person is convicted of a class A drug trafficking offence committed after the commencement of this section;

(b) at the time when that offence was committed, he was 18 or over and had been convicted in any part of the United Kingdom of two other class A drug trafficking offences; and

(c) one of those other offences was committed after he had been convicted of the other.

(2) The court shall impose a custodial sentence for a term of at least seven years except where the court is of the opinion that there are specific circumstances which—

(a) relate to any of the offences or to the offender; and

(b) would make the prescribed custodial sentence unjust in all the circumstances.

(3) Where the court does not impose such a sentence, it shall state in open court that it is of that opinion and what the specific circumstances are.

(4) Where—

(a) a person is charged with a class A drug trafficking offence (which, apart from this subsection, would be triable either way); and

    (b) the circumstances are such that, if he were convicted of the offence, he could be sentenced for it under subsection (2) above,

the offence shall be triable only on indictment.

(5) In this section "class A drug trafficking offence" means a drug trafficking offence committed in respect of a class A drug; and for this purpose—

1971 c.38.

    "class A drug" has the same meaning as in the Misuse of Drugs Act 1971;

1994 c.37.
1995 c.43.
S.I. 1996/1299
(N.I.9).

    "drug trafficking offence" means a drug trafficking offence within the meaning of the Drug Trafficking Act 1994, the Proceeds of Crime (Scotland) Act 1995 or the Proceeds of Crime (Northern Ireland) Order 1996.

(6) In this section and section 4 below "custodial sentence" means—

    (a) in relation to a person who is 21 or over, a sentence of imprisonment;

    (b) in relation to a person who is under 21, a sentence of detention in a young offender institution.

Minimum of three years for third domestic burglary.

4.—(1) This section applies where—

    (a) a person is convicted of a domestic burglary committed after the commencement of this section;

    (b) at the time when that burglary was committed, he was 18 or over and had been convicted in England and Wales of two other domestic burglaries; and

    (c) one of those other burglaries was committed after he had been convicted of the other, and both of them were committed after the commencement of this section.

(2) The court shall impose a custodial sentence for a term of at least three years except where the court is of the opinion that there are specific circumstances which—

    (a) relate to any of the offences or to the offender; and

    (b) would make the prescribed custodial sentence unjust in all the circumstances.

(3) Where the court does not impose such a sentence, it shall state in open court that it is of that opinion and what the specific circumstances are.

(4) Where—

    (a) a person is charged with a domestic burglary which, apart from this subsection, would be triable either way; and

    (b) the circumstances are such that, if he were convicted of the burglary, he could be sentenced for it under subsection (2) above,

the burglary shall be triable only on indictment.

(5) In this section "domestic burglary" means a burglary committed in respect of a building or part of a building which is a dwelling.

5.—(1) This section applies where—

    (a) a sentence has been imposed on any person under subsection (2) of section 2, 3 or 4 above; and

    (b) any previous conviction of his without which that section would not have applied has been subsequently set aside on appeal.

(2) Notwithstanding anything in section 18 of the Criminal Appeal Act 1968, notice of appeal against the sentence may be given at any time within 28 days from the date on which the previous conviction was set aside.

6.—(1) Where—

    (a) on any date after the commencement of this section a person is convicted in England and Wales of a serious offence, a class A drug trafficking offence or a domestic burglary; and

    (b) the court by or before which he is so convicted states in open court that he has been convicted of such an offence on that date; and

    (c) that court subsequently certifies that fact,

the certificate shall be evidence, for the purposes of the relevant section, that he was convicted of such an offence on that date.

(2) Where—

    (a) after the commencement of this section a person is convicted in England and Wales of a class A drug trafficking offence or a domestic burglary; and

    (b) the court by or before which he is so convicted states in open court that the offence was committed on a particular day or over, or at some time during, a particular period; and

    (c) that court subsequently certifies that fact,

the certificate shall be evidence, for the purposes of the relevant section, that the offence was committed on that day or over, or at some time during, that period.

(3) In this section—

    "serious offence", "class A drug trafficking offence" and "domestic burglary" have the same meanings as in sections 2, 3 and 4 respectively; and

    "the relevant section", in relation to any such offence, shall be construed accordingly.

7.—(1) Where—

    (a) a person has at any time been convicted of an offence under section 70 of the Army Act 1955 or the Air Force Act 1955 or section 42 of the Naval Discipline Act 1957; and

    (b) the corresponding civil offence (within the meaning of that Act) was a serious offence, a class A drug trafficking offence or a domestic burglary,

the relevant section shall have effect as if he had at that time been convicted in England and Wales of the corresponding civil offence.

(2) Subsection (3) of section 6 above applies for the purposes of this section as it applies for the purposes of that section.

PART II

EFFECT OF CUSTODIAL SENTENCES

CHAPTER I

DETERMINATE SENTENCES

General

Time to be served.

8.—(1) Subject to the following provisions of this Chapter, a prisoner shall be released when he has served his sentence.

(2) In this Chapter "prisoner" means any person who is sentenced to imprisonment for a term in respect of an offence committed after the commencement of this Chapter.

Crediting of periods of remand in custody.

9.—(1) This section applies where—

(a) a court sentences an offender to imprisonment for a term in respect of an offence committed after the commencement of this section; and

(b) the offender has been remanded in custody in connection with the offence or a related offence, that is to say, any other offence the charge for which was founded on the same facts or evidence.

(2) It is immaterial for that purpose whether the offender—

(a) has also been remanded in custody in connection with other offences; or

(b) has also been detained in connection with other matters.

(3) Subject to subsection (4) below, the court shall direct that the number of days for which the offender was remanded in custody in connection with the offence or a related offence shall count as time served by him as part of the sentence.

(4) Subsection (3) above shall not apply if and to the extent that—

(a) rules made by the Secretary of State so provide in the case of—

(i) a remand in custody which is wholly or partly concurrent with a sentence of imprisonment; or

(ii) sentences of imprisonment for consecutive terms or for terms which are wholly or partly concurrent; or

(b) it is in the opinion of the court just in all the circumstances not to give a direction under that subsection.

(5) Where the court gives a direction under subsection (3) above, it shall state in open court—

(a) the number of days for which the offender was remanded in custody; and

(b) the number of days in relation to which the direction is given.

(6) Where the court does not give a direction under subsection (3) above, or gives such a direction in relation to a number of days less than that for which the offender was remanded in custody, it shall state in open court—

(a) that its decision is in accordance with rules made under paragraph (a) of subsection (4) above; or

(b) that it is of the opinion mentioned in paragraph (b) of that subsection and what the circumstances are.

(7) The power to make rules under subsection (4)(a) above shall be exercisable by statutory instrument; but no such rules shall be made unless a draft of the rules has been laid before and approved by a resolution of each House of Parliament.

(8) For the purposes of this section a suspended sentence shall be treated as a sentence of imprisonment when it takes effect under section 23 of the Powers of Criminal Courts Act 1973 ("the 1973 Act") and as being imposed by the order under which it takes effect.

1973 c.62.

(9) References in this section to an offender being remanded in custody are references to his being—

(a) held in police detention; or

(b) remanded in or committed to custody by an order of a court.

(10) A person is in police detention for the purposes of this section—

(a) at any time when he is in police detention for the purposes of the Police and Criminal Evidence Act 1984; and

1984 c.60.

(b) at any time when he is detained under section 14 of the Prevention of Terrorism (Temporary Provisions) Act 1989.

1989 c.4.

Early release

10.—(1) The Secretary of State may at any time release a prisoner if he is satisfied that exceptional circumstances exist which justify the prisoner's release on compassionate grounds.

Early release on compassionate grounds.

(2) Before releasing under subsection (1) above a prisoner who is serving a sentence of imprisonment for a term of three years or more, the Secretary of State shall consult the Parole Board, unless the circumstances are such as to render such consultation impracticable.

11.—(1) This section applies where a prisoner is serving a sentence of imprisonment for a term of more than two months and less than three years.

Award of early release days for good behaviour.

(2) For each initial assessment period, the prescribed person may award the prisoner such number of early release days, not exceeding twelve, as he may determine having regard to the extent to which the prisoner's behaviour during the period has attained the prescribed minimum standard.

(3) For each subsequent assessment period, the prescribed person may award the prisoner—

(a) such number of early release days, not exceeding six, as he may determine having regard to the extent to which the prisoner's behaviour during the period has attained the prescribed minimum standard; and

(b) such number of such days, not exceeding six, as he may determine having regard to the extent to which the prisoner's behaviour during the period has exceeded that standard.

(4) Where at any time this section applies in place of section 12, 28 or 29 below because a sentence is set aside or varied on appeal, then, for each assessment period for the purposes of this section beginning before that time, the prescribed person shall assume, for the purposes of subsection

(2) or (3) above, that the prisoner's behaviour was such as to entitle him to the maximum number of early release days available under that subsection.

(5) Where any early release days are awarded to a prisoner, any period which he must serve before becoming entitled to be released shall be reduced by the aggregate of those days; but nothing in this subsection shall entitle a prisoner to be released on the basis of an award before the day after that on which the award is made.

(6) Prison rules may—

(a) require determinations under this section to be made at prescribed times, and to be notified to the prisoners concerned in the prescribed manner; and

(b) make provision for enabling prisoners to appeal against such determinations to prescribed persons.

(7) The Secretary of State may by order provide that subsections (2) and (3) above shall have effect subject to such amendments as may be specified in the order; but no amendment so specified shall reduce—

(a) the number of days specified in subsection (2) or (3)(a); or

(b) the total number of days specified in subsection (3).

(8) The power to make an order under this section shall be exercisable by statutory instrument which shall be subject to annulment in pursuance of a resolution of either House of Parliament.

(9) In this section, in relation to a prisoner—

"assessment period" means—

(a) the period of two months beginning with the day on which he was sentenced; and

(b) each successive period of two months ending before his release;

"initial assessment period" means an assessment period beginning less than twelve months after the day on which he was sentenced and "subsequent assessment period" shall be construed accordingly.

Early release on Parole Board recommendation.

12.—(1) This section applies where a prisoner is serving a sentence of imprisonment for a term of three years or more.

(2) As soon as the prisoner has served five-sixths of his sentence, the Secretary of State shall, if recommended to do so by the Parole Board, release him.

Provisional early release days for remand prisoners.

13.—(1) This section applies where an accused is remanded in custody in connection with one or more offences—

(a) which are alleged to have been committed after the commencement of this Chapter; and

(b) in respect of which he would be liable, if convicted, to a life sentence or to imprisonment for a term of more than two months.

(2) For the purpose of enabling early release days to be awarded on a provisional basis, subsections (2) and (3) of section 11 above shall have effect as if—

(a) the accused had been convicted of, or of an offence related to, the offence or any of the offences, and had been sentenced to imprisonment for a term of more than two months and less than three years, on the day on which he was remanded in custody;

(b) any days falling after that day for which he is not remanded in custody were disregarded; and

(c) references in that section to periods of two months were references to periods of 60 days.

(3) Subsections (4) to (6) below shall apply if, and only if, each of the following conditions is fulfilled, namely—

(a) the accused is convicted of, or of an offence related to, the offence or any of the offences;

(b) he is sentenced to imprisonment for a term of more than two months and less than three years; and

(c) a direction is given under section 9 above.

(4) For the purposes of section 11(5) above, any early release days provisionally awarded under subsection (2) above shall be treated as early release days awarded on the day on which the direction under section 9 above is given.

(5) For the purpose of securing that any days for which the accused was remanded in custody are taken into account in determining assessment periods for the purposes of section 11 above, that section shall have effect as if—

(a) the accused had been convicted and sentenced on the day on which he was remanded in custody;

(b) any days which fell before the day on which he was sentenced, and for which he was not remanded in custody, were disregarded; and

(c) references to periods of two months, in their application to periods beginning before that day, were references to periods of 60 days.

(6) If the direction under section 9 above is given in relation to a number of days less than that for which the accused was remanded in custody—

(a) subsection (4) above shall have effect as if the reference to any early release days provisionally awarded under subsection (2) above were a reference to the appropriate proportion of those days (rounded up to the nearest whole day); and

(b) subsection (5) above shall have effect as if the reference to days for which he was not remanded in custody included a reference to the complementary proportion of the days for which he was so remanded (rounded down to the nearest whole day).

(7) Where for any period the accused has been held in police detention, the prescribed person shall assume, for the purposes of section 11(2) and (3) above as modified by subsection (2) above, that during that period—

(a) the prisoner had been in prison; and

(b) his behaviour had attained, but not exceeded, the prescribed minimum standard for the purposes of that section.

(8) In this section—

"the appropriate proportion" means the proportion which the number of days in relation to which the direction under section 9 above is given bears to the number of days for which the accused was remanded in custody, and "the complementary proportion" shall be construed accordingly;

"life sentence" has the same meaning as in section 34 below;

"related", in relation to an offence, has the same meaning as in section 9 above;

and subsections (2), (9) and (10) of section 9 above shall apply for the purposes of this section as they apply for the purposes of that section.

Additional days

14.—(1) Prison rules may include provision for the award of additional days to prisoners who are guilty of disciplinary offences.

(2) Subject to subsection (3) below, where any additional days are awarded to a prisoner, and are not remitted in accordance with prison rules, any period which he must serve before becoming—

(a) entitled to be released under section 11 above; or

(b) eligible to be released under section 12 above,

shall be extended by the aggregate of those days.

(3) Nothing in subsection (2) above shall have the effect of extending any such period beyond the end of the prisoner's sentence, taking into account for this purpose any days directed by the court to count as time served as part of that sentence.

15.—(1) This section applies where an accused is remanded in custody in connection with one or more offences—

(a) which are alleged to have been committed after the commencement of this Chapter; and

(b) in respect of which he would be liable, if convicted, to a life sentence or to imprisonment for a term of more than two months.

(2) For the purpose of enabling additional days to be awarded on a provisional basis, prison rules made by virtue of section 14(1) above shall have effect as if the accused—

(a) had been convicted of, or of an offence related to, the offence or any of the offences; and

(b) had been sentenced to imprisonment for a term of more than two months, on the day on which he was remanded in custody.

(3) Subsections (4) and (5) below shall apply if, and only if, each of the following conditions is fulfilled, namely—

(a) the accused is convicted of, or of an offence related to, the offence or any of the offences;

(b) he is sentenced to imprisonment for a term of more than two months; and

(c) a direction is given under section 9 above.

(4) For the purposes of section 14(2) and (3) above, any additional days provisionally awarded under subsection (2) above shall be treated as additional days awarded on the day on which the direction under section 9 above is given.

(5) If the direction under section 9 above is given in relation to a number of days less than that for which the accused was remanded in custody, subsection (4) above shall have effect as if the reference to any additional days provisionally awarded under subsection (2) above were a reference to the appropriate proportion of those days (rounded up to the nearest whole day).

(6) In this section—

"the appropriate proportion" has the same meaning as in section 13 above;

"life sentence" has the same meaning as in section 34 below;

"related", in relation to an offence, has the same meaning as in section 9 above;

and subsections (2), (9) and (10) of section 9 above shall apply for the purposes of this section as they apply for the purposes of that section.

Supervision after release

16.—(1) This section applies where—

(a) an offender who has been sentenced to imprisonment for a term of twelve months or more in respect of an offence committed after the commencement of this Chapter is released otherwise than under section 10 above;

(b) an offender who has been so sentenced is released under that section; or

(c) an offender who has been sentenced to imprisonment for a term of less than twelve months in respect of an offence committed after that commencement is released under that section.

Release supervision orders.

(2) On his release, the offender shall be subject to a release supervision order—

(a) in a case falling within subsection (1)(a) above, for a period equal to 25 per cent of his term of imprisonment (rounded up to the nearest whole day) or a period of three months, whichever is the greater;

(b) in a case falling within subsection (1)(b) above, for a period equal to the aggregate of the period mentioned in paragraph (a) above and the period mentioned in paragraph (c) below;

(c) in a case falling within subsection (1)(c) above, for a period equal to so much of the remainder of his term as he would have been liable to serve but for his release under section 10 above;

and in applying paragraphs (b) and (c) above account shall be taken of any early release or additional days awarded to the offender before his release.

(3) The release supervision order, which shall be made by the Secretary of State, shall provide that, throughout the period for which the order is in force ("the release supervision period"), the offender, so long as he is at large—

(a) shall be under the supervision of a probation officer; and

(b) shall comply with such conditions as are for the time being specified in the order.

(4) The Secretary of State—

(a) shall not specify any condition which—

(i) requires the offender to live in an approved probation hostel; or

(ii) makes such provision as is made by a curfew order,

except in accordance with recommendations of the Parole Board made after an oral hearing at which the offender had the opportunity to be heard or represented; and

(b) in the case of an offender who has been sentenced to imprisonment for a term of three years or more, shall not specify any other condition except in accordance with recommendations of that Board.

(5) The Secretary of State may make rules for regulating the supervision under this section of any description of offenders.

(6) The power to make rules under this section shall be exercisable by statutory instrument which shall be subject to annulment in pursuance of a resolution of either House of Parliament.

(7) In this section—

"approved probation hostel" has the same meaning as in the Probation Service Act 1993;

1993 c.47.

1991 c.53.

"curfew order" has the same meaning as in the Criminal Justice Act 1991 ("the 1991 Act").

Breach of conditions of release supervision order.

17.—(1) If any offender in respect of whom a release supervision order is in force fails without reasonable excuse to comply with any of the conditions of the order, he shall be liable—

(a) on conviction on indictment, to imprisonment for a term not exceeding the relevant period or a fine or both;

(b) on summary conviction, to imprisonment for a term not exceeding the relevant period or a fine not exceeding level 3 on the standard scale or both.

(2) An offence under subsection (1) above shall not be triable on indictment unless—

(a) the relevant period would be longer than six months; or

(b) the act or omission in question constitutes another offence which is punishable with imprisonment and is triable on indictment.

(3) A magistrates' court by which an offender is convicted of an offence under subsection (1) above which could have been tried on indictment may commit him in custody or on bail to the Crown Court for sentence; and the Crown Court to which he has been so committed may impose on him such a sentence as is mentioned in subsection (1)(a) above.

(4) A court shall not impose a sentence of imprisonment under subsection (1) above unless—

(a) it considers it expedient to do so in the interests of protecting the public from serious harm from the offender; or

(b) the offender's failure to comply with the condition in question consisted of the commission of an offence punishable with imprisonment.

(5) Nothing in section 1 or 2 of the 1991 Act shall apply in relation to such a sentence; and nothing in section 6 of that Act shall prevent a court from dealing with the offender in respect of an offence under subsection (1) above in any one of the following ways, namely—

(a) where the offender is 16 or over—

(i) by making a community service order, probation order or combination order in respect of him; or

(ii) by making a curfew order in respect of him; or

(iii) by doing both of those things;

(b) where the offender is under 18—

(i) by making a supervision order in respect of him; or

(ii) by making both such an order and a curfew order in respect of him; and

(c) where the case is one to which section 17 of the 1982 Act applies—

(i) by making an order under that section requiring the offender to attend at an attendance centre; or

(ii) by making both such an order and a curfew order in respect of him.

(6) In this section—

"combination order" and "curfew order" have the same meanings as in the 1991 Act;

"community service order" and "probation order" have the same meanings as in the 1973 Act;

"supervision order" means a supervision order under the Children and Young Persons Act 1969 ("the 1969 Act"); 1969 c.54.

"the relevant period" means—

(a) on conviction on indictment, so much of the release supervision period as falls after the day on which the offender failed to comply with the condition;

(b) on summary conviction, so much of that period as so falls or six months, whichever is the shorter.

18.—(1) A constable may arrest without warrant any person whom he has reasonable grounds for suspecting to have committed an offence under section 17 above.

Powers of arrest and search warrants.

(2) If a justice of the peace is by written information on oath satisfied that there is reasonable ground for suspecting that a person who is liable to be arrested under subsection (1) above is to be found on any premises, he may grant a warrant authorising any constable to enter, if need be by force, the premises named in the warrant for the purposes of searching for and arresting that person.

(3) Section 8 of the Police and Criminal Evidence Act 1984 (power of justice to authorise entry and search of premises) shall have effect as if the reference in subsection (1) of that section to a serious arrestable offence included a reference to an offence under section 17 above.

1984 c.60.

Special cases

Young offenders.

19.—(1) Subject to the provisions of this section, this Chapter applies to—

  (a) a sentence of detention in a young offender institution; and

1933 c.12.

  (b) a determinate sentence of detention under section 53 of the Children and Young Persons Act 1933 ("the 1933 Act"),

as it applies to an equivalent sentence of imprisonment.

(2) References in this Chapter to prisoners, or to prison or imprisonment, shall be construed in accordance with subsection (1) above.

(3) Section 9 above applies to periods of detention which offenders are liable to serve under secure training orders as it applies to sentences of imprisonment; and sections 9, 13 and 15 above apply to persons—

1980 c.43.

  (a) remanded or committed to local authority accommodation under section 23 of the 1969 Act or section 37 of the Magistrates' Courts Act 1980 ("the 1980 Act"); and

  (b) placed and kept in secure accommodation,

as they apply to persons remanded in or committed to custody by an order of a court.

(4) For each assessment period for the purposes of section 11 above during the whole or part of which the prisoner—

  (a) is under 16; or

1989 c.41.

  (b) is detained in local authority accommodation, or a home provided by the Secretary of State under section 82(5) of the Children Act 1989,

the prescribed person shall assume, for the purposes of subsection (2) or (3) of that section, that the prisoner's behaviour had been such as to entitle him to the maximum number of early release days available under that subsection.

(5) For each assessment period for the purposes of section 13 above during the whole or part of which the accused—

  (a) is under 16; or

  (b) is a person to whom section 9 applies by virtue of subsection (3) above,

the prescribed person shall assume, for the purposes of subsection (2) or (3) of section 11 above as modified by section 13(2) above, that the accused's behaviour had been such as to entitle him to the maximum number of early release days available under that subsection.

(6) In relation to a released offender who is under 22, section 16 above shall have effect as if—

  (a) in subsection (1), paragraph (c) and, in paragraph (a), the words "of twelve months or more" were omitted; and

  (b) in subsection (3)(a), the reference to supervision by a probation officer included a reference to supervision by a social worker of a local authority social services department.

(7) Where a released offender who is under 18 and whose sentence was a determinate sentence of detention under section 53 of the 1933 Act commits an offence under section 17 above, the court may deal with him

as if subsection (3) of section 53 applied; but no sentence of detention imposed by virtue of this subsection shall be for a term exceeding the relevant period within the meaning of section 17 above.

(8) In relation to a released offender who is under 22 and whose sentence—

> (a) was a sentence of detention in a young offender institution, or a sentence of detention under section 53 of the 1933 Act, for a term of less than 12 months; and

> (b) was not imposed in respect of a sexual offence committed after the commencement of this Chapter,

section 17 above shall have effect as if the relevant period for the purposes of that section were a period of 30 days.

(9) Where an offender is released from a sentence of detention imposed under section 17 above as modified by subsection (8) above, he shall not be liable to a release supervision order in consequence of his conviction under that section.

(10) In this section "secure accommodation" has the same meaning as in section 23 of the 1969 Act, and—

> (a) any reference to a sentence of detention in a young offender institution includes a reference to a sentence under a custodial order within the meaning of section 71AA of the Army Act 1955 or the Air Force Act 1955 or section 43AA of the Naval Discipline Act 1957; and

> (b) any reference (however expressed) to a determinate sentence of detention under section 53 of the 1933 Act includes a reference to a sentence of detention under subsection (4) of section 71A of the Army Act 1955 or the Air Force Act 1955 or section 43A of the Naval Discipline Act 1957.

1955 c.18.
1955 c.19.
1957 c.53.

20.—(1) Subsection (2) below applies where—   Sexual offenders.

> (a) there is released under this Chapter an offender who has been sentenced to imprisonment for a term in respect of a sexual offence committed after the commencement of this Chapter; and

> (b) the court by which he was so sentenced gave a direction under subsection (3) below.

(2) Section 16 above shall have effect in relation to the offender as if—

> (a) in subsection (1), paragraph (c) and, in paragraph (a), the words "of twelve months or more" were omitted; and

> (b) for subsection (2) there were substituted the following subsection—

"(2) On his release, the offender shall be subject to a release supervision order—

> (a) where he is released otherwise than under section 10 above, for such period as is specified in the direction under section 20(3) below;

> (b) where he is released under section 10 above, for a period equal to the aggregate of—

>> (i) the period mentioned in paragraph (a) above; and

(ii) a period equal to so much of the remainder of his term as he would have been liable to serve but for his release under section 10 above;

and in applying paragraph (b) above account shall be taken of any early release or additional days awarded to the offender before his release."

(3) Where a court sentences an offender to imprisonment for a term in respect of a sexual offence committed after the commencement of this Chapter, it shall give a direction under this subsection unless it is of the opinion that there are exceptional circumstances which justify its not doing so.

(4) Where the court does not give a direction under subsection (3) above, it shall state in open court that it is of that opinion and what the exceptional circumstances are.

(5) A direction under subsection (3) above shall direct that the offender's release supervision period shall be such period as is specified in the direction.

(6) The period so specified shall be—

(a) a period equal to 50 per cent of the offender's term of imprisonment (rounded up to the nearest whole day) or a period of twelve months, whichever is the longer; or

(b) if the court considers a longer period necessary for the purpose of preventing the commission by the offender of further offences and of securing his rehabilitation, such longer period, not exceeding ten years, as it may determine.

Violent offenders.

21.—(1) Subsection (2) below applies where—

(a) there is released under this Chapter an offender who has been sentenced to imprisonment for a term of three years or more in respect of a violent offence committed after the commencement of this Chapter; and

(b) the court by which he was so sentenced gave a direction under subsection (3) below.

(2) Section 16 above shall have effect in relation to the offender as if for subsection (2) there were substituted the following subsection—

"(2) On his release, the offender shall be subject to a release supervision order—

(a) where he is released otherwise than under section 10 above, for such period as is specified in the direction under section 21(3) below;

(b) where he is released under section 10 above, for a period equal to the aggregate of—

(i) the period mentioned in paragraph (a) above; and

(ii) a period equal to so much of the remainder of his term as he would have been liable to serve but for his release under section 10 above."

(3) Where a court sentences an offender to imprisonment for a term of three years or more in respect of a violent offence committed after the commencement of this Chapter, it may give a direction under this

subsection if it considers a longer release supervision period necessary for the purpose of preventing the commission by the offender of further offences and of securing his rehabilitation.

(4) A direction under subsection (3) above shall direct that the offender's release supervision period shall be such period, not more than 50 per cent of the offender's term of imprisonment, as is specified in the direction.

(5) In this section "violent offence" has the same meaning as in Part I of the 1991 Act.

22.—(1) Subject to subsection (3) below, sections 9 and 13 above apply to persons—

Mentally disordered offenders.

(a) remanded to hospital under section 35 or 36 (remands to hospital) of the Mental Health Act 1983 ("the 1983 Act");

1983 c.20.

(b) admitted to hospital under section 38 of that Act (interim hospital orders); or

(c) removed to hospital under section 48 of that Act (removal to hospital),

as they apply to persons remanded in or committed to custody by an order of a court.

(2) In the case of a prisoner who for any period is detained in a hospital under section 45A of the 1983 Act (power of courts to direct hospital admission), or under section 47 (removal of prisoners to hospital) and section 49 (restriction on discharge of prisoners removed to hospital) of that Act—

(a) section 11 above shall apply as if references to the prescribed person in subsections (2) and (3) were references to the Secretary of State and subsection (6) were omitted; and

(b) the Secretary of State shall assume, for the purposes of subsection (2) or (3) of that section as so modified, that during that period—

(i) the prisoner had been in prison; and

(ii) his behaviour had been such as to entitle him to the maximum number of early release days available under that subsection.

(3) In the case of an accused who for any period is a person to whom section 13 above applies by virtue of subsection (1) above—

(a) that section shall apply as if references to the prescribed person in section 11(2) and (3) above as modified by section 13(2) above were references to the Secretary of State; and

(b) the Secretary of State shall assume, for the purposes of section 11(2) or (3) above as modified by section 13(2) above, that during that period—

(i) the accused had been in prison; and

(ii) his behaviour had been such as to entitle him to the maximum number of early release days available under that subsection.

(4) Where, immediately before the expiration of his sentence, a prisoner is detained in a hospital under section 45A of the 1983 Act, or under section 47 and 49 of that Act, section 16 above shall have effect as if—

(a) the prisoner had been released on the expiration of his sentence;

(b) the reference in subsection (3)(a) to supervision by a probation officer included a reference to supervision by a social worker of a local authority social services department;

(c) the reference in subsection (4)(a) to an approved probation hostel included a reference to any hostel or home whose residents are subject to supervision; and

(d) subsection (4)(b) were omitted.

(5) In this section references to the expiration of the prisoner's sentence shall be construed in accordance with subsection (3) of section 50 of the 1983 Act (prisoners under sentence).

Fine defaulters and contemnors.

23. This Chapter (except sections 16 to 18 above) applies to persons committed to prison or to be detained under section 9 of the 1982 Act—

(a) in default of payment of a sum adjudged to be paid by a conviction; or

(b) for contempt of court or any kindred offence,

as it applies to persons serving equivalent sentences of imprisonment; and references in this Chapter to prisoners, or to prison or imprisonment, shall be construed accordingly.

Persons liable to removal from the United Kingdom.

24.—(1) In relation to an offender who is liable to removal from the United Kingdom—

(a) section 12 above shall have effect as if, in subsection (2), for the words "shall, if recommended to do so by the Parole Board," there were substituted the word "may"; and

(b) section 16 above shall have effect as if, in subsection (2), for the words "On his release, the offender shall" there were substituted the words "If the Secretary of State thinks fit, the offender shall, on his release,".

(2) An offender is liable to removal from the United Kingdom for the purposes of this section if—

1971 c.77.

(a) he is liable to deportation under section 3(5) of the Immigration Act 1971 and has been notified of a decision to make a deportation order against him;

(b) he is liable to deportation under section 3(6) of that Act;

(c) he has been notified of a decision to refuse him leave to enter the United Kingdom; or

(d) he is an illegal entrant within the meaning of section 33(1) of that Act.

Persons extradited to the United Kingdom.

25.—(1) A prisoner is an extradited prisoner for the purposes of this section if—

(a) he was tried for the offence in respect of which his sentence was imposed—

(i) after having been extradited to the United Kingdom; and

(ii) without having first been restored or had an opportunity of leaving the United Kingdom; and

(b) he was kept in custody while awaiting his extradition to the United Kingdom as mentioned in paragraph (a) above.

(2) If, in the case of an extradited prisoner, the court by which he was sentenced so ordered, this Chapter shall have effect in relation to him as if a number of days specified in the order were a number of days in relation to which a direction under section 9 above had been given.

(3) The number of days that may be so specified is such number as in the opinion of the court is just in all the circumstances and does not exceed the number of days for which he was kept in custody as mentioned in subsection (1)(b) above.

(4) In this section—

"extradited to the United Kingdom" means returned to the United Kingdom—

(i) in pursuance of extradition arrangements;

(ii) under any law of a designated Commonwealth country corresponding to the Extradition Act 1989;

        1989 c.33.

(iii) under that Act as extended to a colony or under any corresponding law of a colony;

(iv) in pursuance of a warrant of arrest endorsed in the Republic of Ireland under the law of that country corresponding to the Backing of Warrants (Republic of Ireland) Act 1965; or

        1965 c.45.

(v) in pursuance of arrangements with a foreign state in respect of which an Order in Council under section 2 of the Extradition Act 1870 is in force;

        1970 c.52.

"extradition arrangements" has the meaning given by section 3 of the Extradition Act 1989;

"designated Commonwealth country" has the meaning given by section 5(1) of that Act.

Supplemental

26.—(1) This section has effect for the purpose of securing that, where a person is sentenced to a term of imprisonment in respect of an offence—

        Continuity of sentencing.

(a) to which this section applies; and

(b) which is committed after the commencement of this Chapter,

he serves approximately the same time in prison as he would have served if the offence had been committed immediately before that commencement.

(2) Subject to sections 3(2) and 4(2) above, the court by which a person is so sentenced at any time shall impose a term which is equal to two-thirds of the term which, at that time, it would have considered to be appropriate if the offence had been so committed.

(3) This section applies to any offence other than one—

(a) which did not subsist, or was not punishable with imprisonment, immediately before the commencement of this Chapter; or

(b) for which the maximum sentence of imprisonment that may be imposed has been varied after that commencement.

Interpretation of
Chapter I.

27.—(1) In this Chapter—

"court", except in sections 9, 17 and 19 above, includes a court-martial and a Standing Civilian Court;

"prescribed" means prescribed by prison rules;

1952 c.52.

"prison rules" means rules made under section 47 of the Prison Act 1952;

"prisoner" has the meaning given by section 8(2) above;

"sentence of imprisonment" does not include a committal—

(a) in default of payment of any sum of money;

(b) for want of sufficient distress to satisfy any sum of money; or

(c) for failure to do or abstain from doing anything required to be done or left undone;

and cognate expressions shall be construed accordingly;

"sexual offence" has the same meaning as in Part I of the 1991 Act.

(2) Subject to subsections (3) and (4) below, for the purposes of any reference in this Chapter, however expressed, to the term of imprisonment to which a person has been or could be sentenced, consecutive terms and terms which are wholly or partly concurrent shall be treated as a single term.

(3) Subsection (4) below applies where—

(a) an offender sentenced to two or more concurrent or consecutive terms of imprisonment is released from prison; and

(b) a direction was given under section 20(3) or 21(3) above in respect of one or more of those terms.

(4) The offender's release supervision period shall be equal to the aggregate of the following, namely—

(a) the period which would be applicable if he had been sentenced only to the term or terms in respect of which such a direction was given; and

(b) the period which would be applicable if he had not been sentenced to the following, namely—

(i) the term or terms mentioned in paragraph (a) above; and

(ii) so much of any other term as was concurrent with, or with any part of, the term or any of the terms so mentioned.

(5) Any order, rules or prison rules made under or by virtue of this Chapter may make such incidental, supplemental and consequential provisions as may appear to the Secretary of State to be necessary or expedient.

CHAPTER II

LIFE SENTENCES

Release on licence

28.—(1) A life prisoner is one to whom this section applies if—

    (a) the conditions mentioned in subsection (2) below are fulfilled; or

    (b) he was under 18 at the time when he committed the offence for which his sentence was imposed.

Duty to release certain life prisoners.

(2) The conditions referred to in subsection (1)(a) above are—

    (a) that the prisoner's sentence was imposed for an offence the sentence for which is not fixed by law; and

    (b) that the court by which he was sentenced for that offence ordered that this section should apply to him as soon as he had served a part of his sentence specified in the order.

(3) A part of a sentence specified in an order under subsection (2)(b) above shall be such part as the court considers appropriate taking into account—

    (a) the seriousness of the offence, or the combination of the offence and other offences associated with it; and

    (b) the effect of any direction which it would have given under section 9 above if it had sentenced him to a term of imprisonment.

(4) Where in the case of a life prisoner to whom this section applies the conditions mentioned in subsection (2) above are not fulfilled, the Secretary of State shall direct that this section shall apply to him as soon as he has served a part of his sentence specified in the direction.

(5) As soon as, in the case of a life prisoner to whom this section applies—

    (a) he has served the part of his sentence specified in the order or direction ("the relevant part"); and

    (b) the Parole Board has directed his release under this section,

it shall be the duty of the Secretary of State to release him on licence.

(6) The Parole Board shall not give a direction under subsection (5) above with respect to a life prisoner to whom this section applies unless—

    (a) the Secretary of State has referred the prisoner's case to the Board; and

    (b) the Board is satisfied that it is no longer necessary for the protection of the public that the prisoner should be confined.

(7) A life prisoner to whom this section applies may require the Secretary of State to refer his case to the Parole Board at any time—

    (a) after he has served the relevant part of his sentence; and

    (b) where there has been a previous reference of his case to the Board, after the end of the period of two years beginning with the disposal of that reference; and

    (c) where he is also serving a sentence of imprisonment or detention for a term, after the time when, but for his life sentence, he would be entitled to be released;

and in this subsection "previous reference" means a reference under subsection (6) above or section 32(4) below.

(8) In determining for the purpose of subsection (5) or (7) above whether a life prisoner to whom this section applies has served the relevant part of his sentence, no account shall be taken of any time during which he was unlawfully at large within the meaning of section 49 of the Prison Act 1952.

1952 c.52.

(9) An offence is associated with another for the purposes of this section if it is so associated for the purposes of Part I of the 1991 Act.

Power to release other life prisoners.

29.—(1) If recommended to do so by the Parole Board, the Secretary of State may, after consultation with the Lord Chief Justice together with the trial judge if available, release on licence a life prisoner who is not one to whom section 28 above applies.

(2) The Parole Board shall not make a recommendation under subsection (1) above unless the Secretary of State has referred the particular case, or the class of case to which that case belongs, to the Board for its advice.

Power to release life prisoners on compassionate grounds.

30.—(1) The Secretary of State may at any time release a life prisoner on licence if he is satisfied that exceptional circumstances exist which justify the prisoner's release on compassionate grounds.

(2) Before releasing a life prisoner under subsection (1) above, the Secretary of State shall consult the Parole Board, unless the circumstances are such as to render such consultation impracticable.

Licences and recall

Duration and conditions of licences.

31.—(1) Where a life prisoner is released on licence, the licence shall, unless previously revoked under section 32(1) or (2) below, remain in force until his death.

(2) A life prisoner subject to a licence shall comply with such conditions (which shall include on his release conditions as to his supervision by a probation officer) as may for the time being be specified in the licence; and the Secretary of State may make rules for regulating the supervision of any description of such persons.

(3) The Secretary of State shall not include on release, or subsequently insert, a condition in the licence of a life prisoner, or vary or cancel any such condition, except—

    (a) in the case of the inclusion of a condition in the licence of a life prisoner to whom section 28 above applies, in accordance with recommendations of the Parole Board; and

    (b) in any other case, after consultation with the Board.

(4) For the purposes of subsection (3) above, the Secretary of State shall be treated as having consulted the Parole Board about a proposal to include, insert, vary or cancel a condition in any case if he has consulted the Board about the implementation of proposals of that description generally or in that class of case.

(5) The power to make rules under this section shall be exercisable by statutory instrument which shall be subject to annulment in pursuance of a resolution of either House of Parliament.

(6) In relation to a life prisoner who is liable to removal from the United Kingdom (within the meaning given by section 24(2) above), subsection (2) above shall have effect as if the words in parentheses were omitted.

32.—(1) If recommended to do so by the Parole Board in the case of a life prisoner who has been released on licence under this Chapter, the Secretary of State may revoke his licence and recall him to prison. Recall of life prisoners while on licence.

(2) The Secretary of State may revoke the licence of any life prisoner and recall him to prison without a recommendation by the Parole Board, where it appears to him that it is expedient in the public interest to recall that person before such a recommendation is practicable.

(3) A life prisoner recalled to prison under subsection (1) or (2) above—

(a) may make representations in writing with respect to his recall; and

(b) on his return to prison, shall be informed of the reasons for his recall and of his right to make representations.

(4) The Secretary of State shall refer to the Parole Board—

(a) the case of a life prisoner recalled under subsection (1) above who makes representations under subsection (3) above; and

(b) the case of a life prisoner recalled under subsection (2) above.

(5) Where on a reference under subsection (4) above the Parole Board—

(a) directs in the case of a life prisoner to whom section 28 above applies; or

(b) recommends in the case of any other life prisoner,

his immediate release on licence under this section, the Secretary of State shall give effect to the direction or recommendation.

(6) On the revocation of the licence of any life prisoner under this section, he shall be liable to be detained in pursuance of his sentence and, if at large, shall be deemed to be unlawfully at large.

Miscellaneous and supplemental

33.—(1) This section applies where, in the case of a transferred life prisoner, the Secretary of State, after consultation with the Lord Chief Justice, certifies his opinion that, if— Life prisoners transferred to England and Wales.

(a) the prisoner's offence had been committed after the commencement of this Chapter; and

(b) he had been sentenced for it in England and Wales,

the court by which he was so sentenced would have ordered that section 28 above should apply to him as soon as he had served a part of his sentence specified in the certificate.

(2) This section also applies where, in the case of a transferred life prisoner, the Secretary of State certifies his opinion that, if—

    (a) the prisoner's offence had been committed after the commencement of this Chapter; and

    (b) he had been sentenced for it in England and Wales,

the Secretary of State would have directed that section 28 above should apply to him as soon as he had served a part of his sentence specified in the certificate.

    (3) In a case to which this section applies, this Chapter except section 29(1) above shall apply as if—

    (a) the transferred life prisoner were a life prisoner to whom section 28 above applies; and

    (b) the relevant part of his sentence within the meaning of section 28 above were the part specified in the certificate.

    (4) In this section "transferred life prisoner" means a person—

    (a) on whom a court in a country or territory outside England and Wales has imposed one or more sentences of imprisonment or detention for an indeterminate period; and

    (b) who has been transferred to England and Wales, in pursuance of—

        (i) an order made by the Secretary of State under paragraph 1 of Schedule 1 to this Act or section 2 of the Colonial Prisoners Removal Act 1884; or

1884 c.31.

        (ii) a warrant issued by the Secretary of State under the Repatriation of Prisoners Act 1984,

1984 c.47.

there to serve his sentence or sentences or the remainder of his sentence or sentences.

    (5) A person who is required so to serve the whole or part of two or more such sentences shall not be treated as a life prisoner to whom section 28 above applies unless the requirements of subsection (1) or (2) above are satisfied as respects each of those sentences; and subsections (5) and (7) of section 28 above shall not apply in relation to such a person until after he has served the relevant part of each of those sentences.

Interpretation of Chapter II.

    34.—(1) In this Chapter "life prisoner" means a person serving one or more life sentences; but—

    (a) a person serving two or more such sentences shall not be treated as a life prisoner to whom section 28 above applies unless the requirements of section 28(1) above are satisfied as respects each of those sentences; and

    (b) subsections (5) and (7) of that section shall not apply in relation to such a person until after he has served the relevant part of each of those sentences.

    (2) In this section "life sentence" means any of the following imposed for an offence, whether committed before or after the commencement of this Chapter, namely—

    (a) a sentence of imprisonment for life;

    (b) a sentence of detention during Her Majesty's pleasure or for life under section 53 of the 1933 Act; and

    (c) a sentence of custody for life under section 8 of the 1982 Act.

(3) In this Chapter "court" includes a court-martial and "trial judge" includes a trial judge advocate; and in subsection (2) above—

   (a) the reference to section 53 of the 1933 Act includes a reference to subsections (3) and (4) of section 71A of the Army Act 1955 and the Air Force Act 1955 and section 43A of the Naval Discipline Act 1957; and

   (b) the reference to section 8 of the 1982 Act includes a reference to subsections (1A) and (1B) of those sections.

1955 c.18.
1955 c.19.
1957 c.53.

PART III

MISCELLANEOUS AND SUPPLEMENTAL

Community sentences

35.—(1) Subsection (2) below applies in any case where a magistrates' court—

   (a) has power under Part III of the 1980 Act to issue a warrant of commitment for default in paying a sum adjudged to be paid by a conviction of a magistrates' court (other than a sum ordered to be paid under section 71 of the Criminal Justice Act 1988 or section 2 of the Drug Trafficking Act 1994); or

   (b) would, but for section 1 of the 1982 Act (restrictions on custodial sentences for persons under 21), have power to issue such a warrant for such default.

Fine defaulters: general.

1988 c.33.
1994 c.37.

(2) The magistrates' court may—

   (a) subject to subsections (4) to (6) and (11) below, make a community service order; or

   (b) subject to subsections (7) to (11) below, make a curfew order,

in respect of the person in default instead of issuing a warrant of commitment or, as the case may be, proceeding under section 81 of the 1980 Act (enforcement of fines imposed on young offenders).

(3) Where a magistrates' court has power to make an order under subsection (2)(a) or (b) above, it may, if it thinks it expedient to do so, postpone the making of the order until such time and on such conditions, if any, as it thinks just.

(4) In this section "community service order" has the same meaning as in the 1973 Act and—

   (a) section 14(2) of that Act; and

   (b) so far as applicable, the other provisions of that Act relating to community service orders and the provisions of Part I of the 1991 Act so relating,

shall have effect in relation to an order under subsection (2)(a) above as they have effect in relation to an order in respect of an offender, but subject to the exceptions in subsection (5) below.

(5) The following are the exceptions, namely—

   (a) the reference in section 14(1A)(a) of the 1973 Act to 40 hours shall be construed as a reference to 20 hours;

   (b) section 14(3) of that Act shall not apply;

(c) the requirements in the order under subsection (2)(a) above shall, as far as practicable, be such as to avoid any interference with the times, if any, at which the offender normally works or attends school or other educational establishment;

(d) the power conferred by paragraph 3(1)(d) of Schedule 2 to the 1991 Act shall be construed as a power to revoke the order or deal with the person in respect of whom the order was made for his default in paying the sum in question or do both of those things; and

(e) paragraph 3(2)(a) of that Schedule shall not apply.

(6) In the case of an amount in default which is described in the first column of the following Table, the period of community service specified in an order under subsection (2)(a) above shall not exceed the number of hours set out opposite that amount in the second column of that Table.

TABLE

Amount	Number of hours
An amount not exceeding £200	40 hours
An amount exceeding £200 but not exceeding £500	60 hours
An amount exceeding £500	100 hours

(7) In this section "curfew order" has the same meaning as in Part I of the 1991 Act and—

(a) section 12(5) of that Act; and

(b) so far as applicable, the other provisions of that Part relating to curfew orders,

shall have effect in relation to an order under subsection (2)(b) above as they have effect in relation to an order in respect of an offender, but subject to the exceptions in subsection (8) below.

(8) The following are the exceptions, namely—

(a) the power conferred by paragraph 3(1)(d) of Schedule 2 to the 1991 Act to revoke the order and deal with an offender for the offence in respect of which the order was made shall be construed as a power to revoke the order or deal with the person in respect of whom the order was made for his default in paying the sum in question or do both of those things; and

(b) paragraph 3(2)(a) of that Schedule shall not apply.

(9) In the case of an amount in default which is described in the first column of the following Table, the number of days to which an order under subsection (2)(b) above relates shall not exceed the number of days set out opposite that amount in the second column of that Table.

TABLE

Amount	Number of days
An amount not exceeding £200	20 days
An amount exceeding £200 but not exceeding £500	30 days
An amount exceeding £500 but not exceeding £1,000	60 days

An amount exceeding £1,000 but not 90 days
  exceeding £2,500

An amount exceeding £2,500 180 days

(10) A magistrates' court shall not make an order under subsection (2)(b) above in respect of a person who is under 16.

(11) A magistrates court shall not make an order under subsection (2)(a) or (b) above unless the court has been notified by the Secretary of State that arrangements for implementing such orders are available in the relevant area and the notice has not been withdrawn.

(12) In subsection (11) above "the relevant area" means—

  (a) in relation to an order under subsection (2)(a) above, the area proposed to be specified in the order;

  (b) in relation to an order under subsection (2)(b) above, the area in which the place proposed to be specified in the order is situated.

(13) Where an order has been made under subsection (2)(a) or (b) above for default in paying any sum—

  (a) on payment of the whole sum to any person authorised to receive it, the order shall cease to have effect;

  (b) on payment of a part of that sum to any such person, the total number of hours or days to which the order relates shall be reduced proportionately;

and the total number is so reduced if it is reduced by such number of complete hours or days as bears to the total number the proportion most nearly approximating to, without exceeding, the proportion which the part paid bears to the whole sum.

(14) The Secretary of State may by order direct that subsection (5)(a), (6) or (9) above shall be amended by substituting for any number of hours or days there specified such number of hours or days as may be specified in the order.

(15) The power to make an order under this section shall be exercisable by statutory instrument; but no such order shall be made unless a draft of the order has been laid before and approved by a resolution of each House of Parliament.

36.—(1) In subsection (1) of section 17 of the 1982 Act (attendance centre orders), after paragraph (b) there shall be inserted the words "or

  (c) has power to commit to prison for default in payment of any sum of money a person who is under 25 but is not less than 21 years of age,".

Fine defaulters under 25.

(2) In subsection (5) of that section, after the words "under 21" there shall be inserted the words "or, as the case may be, 25".

37.—(1) This section applies where—

  (a) a person is convicted of an offence by a magistrates' court or before the Crown Court;

  (b) the court is satisfied that each of the conditions mentioned in subsection (2) below is fulfilled; and

  (c) if it were not so satisfied, the court would be minded to impose a fine in respect of the offence.

Persistent petty offenders.

(2) The conditions are—

    (a) that one or more fines imposed on the offender in respect of one or more previous offences have not been paid; and

    (b) if a fine were imposed in an amount which was commensurate with the seriousness of the offence, the offender would not have sufficient means to pay it.

(3) Notwithstanding anything in section 6 of the 1991 Act, the court may—

    (a) subject to subsections (4) and (6) below, make a community service order; or

    (b) subject to subsections (5) and (6) below, make a curfew order,

in respect of the offender instead of imposing a fine.

(4) Subsections (4) and (5) of section 35 above shall apply for the purposes of this section as they apply for the purposes of that section except that—

    (a) the reference in subsection (4) to subsection (2)(a) of that section shall be construed as a reference to subsection (3)(a) of this section;

    (b) paragraph (a) of subsection (5) shall not apply; and

    (c) the reference in paragraph (d) of that subsection to dealing with the person in respect of whom the order was made for his default in paying the sum in question shall be construed as a reference to dealing with the offender for the offence in respect of which the order was made.

(5) Subsections (7), (8) and (10) of section 35 above shall apply for the purposes of this section as they apply for the purposes of that section except that the references in subsections (7) and (10) to subsection (2)(b) of that section shall be construed as references to subsection (3)(b) of this section.

(6) A court shall not make an order under subsection (3)(a) or (b) above unless the court has been notified by the Secretary of State that arrangements for implementing such orders are available in the relevant area and the notice has not been withdrawn.

(7) In subsection (6) above "the relevant area" means—

    (a) in relation to an order under subsection (3)(a) above, the area proposed to be specified in the order;

    (b) in relation to an order under subsection (3)(b) above, the area in which the place proposed to be specified in the order is situated.

Abolition of certain consent etc. requirements.

38.—(1) In subsection (6) of section 12A of the 1969 Act (young offenders), for paragraph (c) there shall be substituted the following paragraph—

    "(c) if the supervised person is under the age of sixteen, it has obtained and considered information about his family circumstances and the likely effect of the requirements on those circumstances."

(2) The following provisions shall cease to have effect, namely—

    (a) in subsection (3) of section 2 of the 1973 Act (probation orders), the words from "and the court" to the end;

(b) in subsection (2) of section 14 of that Act (community service orders), the words "the offender consents and"; and

(c) in subsection (5) of section 12 of the 1991 Act (curfew orders), the words from "and the court" to the end.

(3) For sub-paragraph (4) of paragraph 5 of Schedule 1A to the 1973 Act (requirements as to treatment for mental condition etc) there shall be substituted the following sub-paragraph—

"(4) A court shall not by virtue of this paragraph include in a probation order a requirement that the offender shall submit to treatment for his mental condition unless—

(a) it is satisfied that arrangements have been made for the treatment intended to be specified in the order (including arrangements for the reception of the offender where he is to be required to submit to treatment as a resident patient); and

(b) the offender has expressed his willingness to comply with such a requirement."

(4) For sub-paragraph (4) of paragraph 6 of that Schedule (requirements as to treatment for drug or alcohol dependency) there shall be substituted the following sub-paragraph—

"(4) A court shall not by virtue of this paragraph include in a probation order a requirement that the offender shall submit to treatment for his dependency on drugs or alcohol unless—

(a) it is satisfied that arrangements have been made for the treatment intended to be specified in the order (including arrangements for the reception of the offender where he is to be required to submit to treatment as a resident patient); and

(b) the offender has expressed his willingness to comply with such a requirement."

Driving disqualifications

39.—(1) Subject to subsections (2) and (3) below, the court by or before which a person is convicted of an offence may, in addition to or instead of dealing with him in any other way, order him to be disqualified, for such period as it thinks fit, for holding or obtaining a driving licence.

Offenders.

(2) Where the person is convicted of an offence the sentence for which is fixed by law or falls to be imposed under section 2(2), 3(2), or 4(2) above, subsection (1) above shall have effect as if the words "or instead of" were omitted.

(3) A court shall not make an order under subsection (1) above unless the court has been notified by the Secretary of State that the power to make such orders is exercisable by the court and the notice has not been withdrawn.

(4) A court which makes an order under this section disqualifying a person for holding or obtaining a driving licence shall require him to produce any such licence held by him together with its counterpart.

PART III

(5) The following provisions, namely—

1988 c.52.

   (a) section 164(5) of the Road Traffic Act 1988 (power of constables to require production of driving licence etc.); and

1988 c.53.

   (b) section 27(3) of the Road Traffic Offenders Act 1988 (failure to produce driving licence),

shall have effect as if the reference to section 44 of the 1973 Act included a reference to this section.

(6) In this section—

"counterpart", in relation to a driving licence, has the meaning given by section 108(1) of the Road Traffic Act 1988;

"driving licence" means a licence to drive a motor vehicle granted under Part III of that Act.

Fine defaulters.

40.—(1) This section applies in any case where a magistrates' court—

   (a) has power under Part III of the 1980 Act to issue a warrant of commitment for default in paying a sum adjudged to be paid by a conviction of a magistrates' court (other than a sum ordered

1988 c.33.
1994 c.37.

      to be paid under section 71 of the Criminal Justice Act 1988 or section 2 of the Drug Trafficking Act 1994); or

   (b) would, but for section 1 of the 1982 Act (restrictions on custodial sentences for persons under 21), have power to issue such a warrant for such default.

(2) Subject to subsection (3) below, the magistrates' court may, instead of issuing a warrant of commitment or, as the case may be, proceeding under section 81 of the 1980 Act (enforcement of fines imposed on young offenders), order the person in default to be disqualified, for such period not exceeding twelve months as it thinks fit, for holding or obtaining a driving licence.

(3) A magistrates court shall not make an order under subsection (2) above unless the court has been notified by the Secretary of State that the power to make such orders is exercisable by the court and the notice has not been withdrawn.

(4) Where an order has been made under subsection (2) above for default in paying any sum—

   (a) on payment of the whole sum to any person authorised to receive it, the order shall cease to have effect;

   (b) on payment of a part of that sum to any such person, the number of weeks or months to which the order relates shall be reduced proportionately;

and the total number is so reduced if it is reduced by such number of complete weeks or months as bears to the total number the proportion most nearly approximating to, without exceeding, the proportion which the part paid bears to the whole sum.

(5) The Secretary of State may by order made by statutory instrument vary the period specified in subsection (2) above; but no such order shall be made unless a draft of the order has been laid before and approved by a resolution of each House of Parliament.

(6) Subsections (4) to (6) of section 39 above shall apply for the purposes of this section as they apply for the purposes of that section.

Transfer and repatriation of prisoners

41. Schedule 1 to this Act (which makes provision with respect to the transfer of prisoners within the British Islands) shall have effect.

42. Schedule 2 to this Act (which makes provision, including retrospective provision, with respect to prisoners repatriated to the British Islands) shall have effect.

Young offenders

43.—(1) In subsection (1) of section 12 of the 1991 Act (curfew orders), the words "of or over the age of sixteen years" shall cease to have effect.

(2) After subsection (2) of that section there shall be inserted the following subsection—

"(2A) In relation to an offender who is under the age of sixteen years, subsection (2)(a) above shall have effect as if the reference to six months were a reference to three months."

(3) After subsection (6) of that section there shall be inserted the following subsection—

"(6A) Before making a curfew order in respect of an offender who is under the age of sixteen years, the court shall obtain and consider information about his family circumstances and the likely effect of such an order on those circumstances."

(4) In paragraph 3(1) of Schedule 2 to the 1991 Act (enforcement of community orders), for paragraph (c) there shall be substituted the following paragraph—

"(c) where—

(i) the relevant order is a probation order, or

(ii) the relevant order is a curfew order and the offender is under the age of sixteen years,

and the case is one to which section 17 of the 1982 Act applies, it may make an order under that section requiring him to attend at an attendance centre; or".

44. In subsection (2)(a) of section 53 of the 1933 Act (long term detention of children and young persons for certain grave crimes), for sub-paragraph (ii) there shall be substituted the following sub-paragraph—

"(ii) an offence under section 14 (indecent assault on a woman) or section 15 (indecent assault on a man) of the Sexual Offences Act 1956;".

45.—(1) After subsection (4) of section 49 of the 1933 Act (restrictions on reports of proceedings in which children or young persons are concerned) there shall be inserted the following subsections—

"(4A) If a court is satisfied that it is in the public interest to do so, it may, in relation to a child or young person who has been convicted of an offence, by order dispense to any specified extent with the requirements of this section in relation to any proceedings before it to which this section applies by virtue of subsection (2)(a) or (b) above, being proceedings relating to—

(a) the prosecution or conviction of the offender for the offence;

(b) the manner in which he, or his parent or guardian, should be dealt with in respect of the offence;

(c) the enforcement, amendment, variation, revocation or discharge of any order made in respect of the offence;

(d) where an attendance centre order is made in respect of the offence, the enforcement of any rules made under section 16(3) of the Criminal Justice Act 1982; or

1982 c.48.

(e) where a secure training order is so made, the enforcement of any requirements imposed under section 3(7) of the Criminal Justice and Public Order Act 1994.

1994 c.33.

(4B) A court shall not exercise its power under subsection (4A) above without—

(a) affording the parties to the proceedings an opportunity to make representations; and

(b) taking into account any representations which are duly made."

(2) Subsection (1) above shall not apply where the offence was committed before the commencement of this section.

Mentally disordered offenders

Power to make hospital and limitation directions.

46. After section 45 of the 1983 Act there shall be inserted the following sections—

"Hospital and limitation directions

Power of higher courts to direct hospital admission.

45A.—(1) This section applies where, in the case of a person convicted before the Crown Court of an offence the sentence for which is not fixed by law—

(a) the conditions mentioned in subsection (2) below are fulfilled; and

(b) except where the offence is one the sentence for which falls to be imposed under section 2 of the Crime (Sentences) Act 1997, the court considers making a hospital order in respect of him before deciding to impose a sentence of imprisonment ("the relevant sentence") in respect of the offence.

(2) The conditions referred to in subsection (1) above are that the court is satisfied, on the written or oral evidence of two registered medical practitioners—

(a) that the offender is suffering from psychopathic disorder;

(b) that the mental disorder from which the offender is suffering is of a nature or degree which makes it appropriate for him to be detained in a hospital for medical treatment; and

(c) that such treatment is likely to alleviate or prevent a deterioration of his condition.

(3) The court may give both of the following directions, namely—

  (a) a direction that, instead of being removed to and detained in a prison, the offender be removed to and detained in such hospital as may be specified in the direction (in this Act referred to as a "hospital direction"); and

  (b) a direction that the offender be subject to the special restrictions set out in section 41 above (in this Act referred to as a "limitation direction").

(4) A hospital direction and a limitation direction shall not be given in relation to an offender unless at least one of the medical practitioners whose evidence is taken into account by the court under subsection (2) above has given evidence orally before the court.

(5) A hospital direction and a limitation direction shall not be given in relation to an offender unless the court is satisfied on the written or oral evidence of the registered medical practitioner who would be in charge of his treatment, or of some other person representing the managers of the hospital that arrangements have been made—

  (a) for his admission to that hospital; and

  (b) for his admission to it within the period of 28 days beginning with the day of the giving of such directions;

and the court may, pending his admission within that period, give such directions as it thinks fit for his conveyance to and detention in a place of safety.

(6) If within the said period of 28 days it appears to the Secretary of State that by reason of an emergency or other special circumstances it is not practicable for the patient to be received into the hospital specified in the hospital direction, he may give instructions for the admission of the patient to such other hospital as appears to be appropriate instead of the hospital so specified.

(7) Where such instructions are given—

  (a) the Secretary of State shall cause the person having the custody of the patient to be informed, and

  (b) the hospital direction shall have effect as if the hospital specified in the instructions were substituted for the hospital specified in the hospital direction.

(8) Section 38(1) and (5) and section 39 above shall have effect as if any reference to the making of a hospital order included a reference to the giving of a hospital direction and a limitation direction.

(9) A hospital direction and a limitation direction given in relation to an offender shall have effect not only as regards the relevant sentence but also (so far as

applicable) as regards any other sentence of imprisonment imposed on the same or a previous occasion.

(10) The Secretary of State may by order provide that this section shall have effect as if the reference in subsection (2) above to psychopathic disorder included a reference to a mental disorder of such other description as may be specified in the order.

(11) An order made under this section may—

    (a) apply generally, or in relation to such classes of offenders or offences as may be specified in the order;

    (b) provide that any reference in this section to a sentence of imprisonment, or to a prison, shall include a reference to a custodial sentence, or to an institution, of such description as may be so specified; and

    (c) include such supplementary, incidental or consequential provisions as appear to the Secretary of State to be necessary or expedient.

Effect of hospital and limitation directions.

45B.—(1) A hospital direction and a limitation direction shall be sufficient authority—

    (a) for a constable or any other person directed to do so by the court to convey the patient to the hospital specified in the hospital direction within a period of 28 days; and

    (b) for the managers of the hospital to admit him at any time within that period and thereafter detain him in accordance with the provisions of this Act.

(2) With respect to any person—

    (a) a hospital direction shall have effect as a transfer direction; and

    (b) a limitation direction shall have effect as a restriction direction.

(3) While a person is subject to a hospital direction and a limitation direction the responsible medical officer shall at such intervals (not exceeding one year) as the Secretary of State may direct examine and report to the Secretary of State on that person; and every report shall contain such particulars as the Secretary of State may require."

Power to specify hospital units.

47.—(1) Subject to subsection (2) below, any power to specify a hospital which is conferred by—

    (a) section 37 of the 1983 Act (hospital orders);

    (b) section 45A of that Act (hospital and limitation directions);

    (c) section 47 of that Act (transfer directions); or

    (d) paragraph 1 of Schedule 1 to the Criminal Procedure (Insanity and Unfitness to Plead) Act 1991 (orders for admission to hospital),

includes power to specify a hospital unit; and where such a unit is specified in relation to any person in the exercise of such a power, any reference in any enactment (including one contained in this Act) to him being, or being liable to be, detained in a hospital shall be construed accordingly.

    (2) In subsection (1) above—

    (a) paragraph (a) shall not apply unless the court also makes an order under section 41 of the 1983 Act (restriction orders);

    (b) paragraph (c) shall not apply unless the Secretary of State also gives a direction under section 49 of that Act (restriction directions); and

    (c) paragraph (d) shall not apply unless the court has given a direction under paragraph 2(1)(b) of Schedule 1 to the Criminal Procedure (Insanity and Unfitness to Plead) Act 1991.

    (3) In this section—

    "hospital", in relation to any exercise of a power, has the same meaning as in the enactment which confers the power;

    "hospital unit" means any part of a hospital which is treated as a separate unit.

    (4) In this section—

    (a) the reference to paragraph 1 of Schedule 1 to the Criminal Procedure (Insanity and Unfitness to Plead) Act 1991 includes a reference to subsection (1) of section 116B of the Army Act 1955 and the Air Force Act 1955 and section 63B of the Naval Discipline Act 1957; and

    (b) the reference to paragraph 2(1)(b) of that Schedule includes a reference to subsection (2) of those sections.

48.—(1) The 1983 Act and the 1984 Act shall have effect subject to the amendments specified in Schedule 3 to this Act, being amendments making provision with respect to transfers within the British Islands of responsibility for offenders conditionally discharged from hospital.

    (2) In this section and that Schedule "the 1984 Act" means the Mental Health (Scotland) Act 1984.

49.—(1) In subsection (5) of section 38 of the 1983 Act (interim hospital orders), for the words "six months" there shall be substituted the words "twelve months".

    (2) In subsection (3) of section 41 of that Act (power of higher courts to restrict discharge from hospital), in paragraph (c)(ii), after the words "section 19 above" there shall be inserted the words "or in pursuance of subsection (3) of that section".

    (3) In subsection (1) of section 47 of that Act (removal to hospital of persons serving sentences of imprisonment etc.), the words "(not being a mental nursing home)" shall cease to have effect.

    (4) In paragraph 5 of Part II of Schedule 1 to that Act (patients subject to hospital and guardianship orders)—

PART III

(a) the word "and" immediately following sub-paragraph (a) shall cease to have effect; and

(b) after sub-paragraph (b) there shall be inserted the words "and

(c) in subsection (3) after the words "may at any time" there shall be inserted the words ", with the consent of the Secretary of State,"."

Miscellaneous

Disclosure of pre-sentence reports.

50.—(1) This section applies where a court obtains a pre-sentence report within the meaning of Part I of the 1991 Act.

(2) Subject to subsections (3) and (4) below, the court shall give a copy of the report—

(a) to the offender or his counsel or solicitor; and

(b) to the prosecutor, that is to say, the person having the conduct of the proceedings in respect of the offence.

(3) If the offender is under 17 and is not represented by counsel or a solicitor, a copy of the report need not be given to him but shall be given to his parent or guardian if present in court.

(4) If the prosecutor is not of a description prescribed by order made by the Secretary of State, a copy of the report need not be given to the prosecutor if the court considers that it would be inappropriate for him to be given it.

(5) No information obtained by virtue of subsection (2)(b) above shall be used or disclosed otherwise than for the purpose of—

(a) determining whether representations as to matters contained in the report need to be made to the court; or

(b) making such representations to the court.

(6) The power to make orders under this section shall be exercisable by statutory instrument which shall be subject to annulment in pursuance of a resolution of either House of Parliament.

Committals for sentence.

51. After section 38 of the 1980 Act there shall be inserted the following section—

"Committal for sentence on indication of guilty plea to offence triable either way.

38A.—(1) This section applies where—

(a) a person who is 18 or over appears or is brought before a magistrates' court ('the court') on an information charging him with an offence triable either way ('the offence');

(b) he or his representative indicates that he would plead guilty if the offence were to proceed to trial; and

(c) proceeding as if section 9(1) above was complied with and he pleaded guilty under it, the court convicts him of the offence.

(2) If the court has committed the offender to the Crown Court for trial for one or more related offences, that is to say, one or more offences which, in its opinion, are related to the offence, it may, in accordance with section 56 of the Criminal Justice Act 1967, commit him

in custody or on bail to the Crown Court to be dealt with in respect of the offence in accordance with the provisions of section 42 of the Powers of Criminal Courts Act 1973.

(3) If the power conferred by subsection (2) above is not exercisable but the court is still to inquire, as examining justices, into one or more related offences—

> (a) it shall adjourn the proceedings relating to the offence until after the conclusion of its inquiries; and

> (b) if it commits the offender to the Crown Court for trial for one or more related offences, it may then exercise that power.

(4) Where the court—

> (a) commits the offender to the Crown Court to be dealt with in respect of the offence; and

> (b) does not state that, in its opinion, it also has power so to commit him under section 38(2) above,

the provisions of section 42 of the Powers of Criminal Courts Act 1973 shall not apply unless he is convicted before the Crown Court of one or more of the related offences.

(5) Where those provisions of that section do not apply, the Crown Court shall have power to deal with the offender in respect of the offence in any manner in which the court might have dealt with him.

(6) For the purposes of this section one offence is related to another if, were they both to be prosecuted on indictment, the charges for them could be joined in the same indictment."

52. In subsection (1) of section 1 of the Indecency with Children Act 1960 (indecent conduct towards young child), for the words "two years" there shall be substituted the words "ten years".

Increased penalty for offence of indecency with children.
1960 c.33.

Supplemental

53. There shall be paid out of money provided by Parliament any increase attributable to this Act in the sums payable out of money so provided under any other Act.

Financial provisions.

54.—(1) In this Act—

"the 1933 Act" means the Children and Young Persons Act 1933;

"the 1969 Act" means the Children and Young Persons Act 1969;

"the 1973 Act" means the Powers of Criminal Courts Act 1973;

"the 1980 Act" means the Magistrates' Courts Act 1980;

"the 1982 Act" means the Criminal Justice Act 1982;

"the 1983 Act" means the Mental Health Act 1983;

"the 1991 Act" means the Criminal Justice Act 1991.

General interpretation.
1933 c.12.
1969 c.54.
1973 c.62.
1980 c.43.
1982 c.48.
1983 c.20.
1991 c.53.

PART III

(2) Any reference in this Act to the commencement of Chapter I of Part II of this Act is a reference to the commencement of the provisions of that Chapter other than sections 9, 20 and 21 above.

(3) Where an offence is found to have been committed over a period of two or more days, or at some time during a period of two or more days, it shall be taken for the purposes of this Act to have been committed on the last of those days.

Minor and consequential amendments.

55.—(1) The enactments mentioned in Schedule 4 to this Act shall have effect subject to the amendments there specified, being minor amendments and amendments consequential on the provisions of this Act.

(2) For the purposes of any of those enactments as so amended—

(a) a sentence falls to be imposed under subsection (2) of section 2, 3 or 4 above if it is required by that subsection in any case where the court is not of the opinion there mentioned; and

1955 c.18.
1955 c.19.
1957 c.53.

(b) a sentence falls to be imposed under subsection (3A) of section 70 of the Army Act 1955 or the Air Force Act 1955 or subsection (1A) of section 42 of the Naval Discipline Act 1957 if it is required by that subsection in any case where the court-martial is not of the opinion there mentioned.

Transitional provisions, savings and repeals.
1978 c.30.

56.—(1) The transitional provisions and savings contained in Schedule 5 to this Act shall have effect; but nothing in this subsection shall be taken as prejudicing the operation of sections 16 and 17 of the Interpretation Act 1978 (which relate to the effect of repeals).

(2) The enactments specified in Schedule 6 to this Act are hereby repealed to the extent specified in the third column of that Schedule.

Short title, commencement and extent.

57.—(1) This Act may be cited as the Crime (Sentences) Act 1997.

(2) This Act shall come into force on such day as the Secretary of State may by order made by statutory instrument appoint; and different days may be appointed for different purposes.

(3) Without prejudice to the provisions of Schedule 5 to this Act, an order under subsection (2) above may make such transitional provisions and savings as appear to the Secretary of State necessary or expedient in connection with any provision brought into force by the order.

(4) Subject to subsections (5) to (8) below, this Act extends to England and Wales only.

(5) The following provisions of this Act extend to Scotland, Northern Ireland and the Channel Islands, namely—

(a) section 41 and Schedule 1; and

1961 c.39.

(b) section 56(2) and Schedule 6 so far as relating to the repeal of Part III of the Criminal Justice Act 1961.

(6) The following provisions of this Act extend to Scotland, namely—

(a) section 45;

(b) paragraphs 1 and 5 to 8 of Schedule 2 and section 42 so far as relating to those paragraphs;

(c) paragraphs 1 and 6 to 10 of Schedule 3 and section 48 so far as relating to those paragraphs;

(d) paragraph 16 of Schedule 4 to this Act and section 55 so far as relating to that paragraph; and

(e) paragraphs 9, 11 and 12 of Schedule 5 and section 56(1) so far as relating to those paragraphs.

(7) The following provisions of this Act extend to Northern Ireland, namely—

(a) paragraphs 1, 9 and 10 of Schedule 2 and section 42 so far as relating to those paragraphs;

(b) paragraphs 2, 3, 7 and 8 of Schedule 3 and section 48 so far as relating to those paragraphs; and

(c) paragraphs 10 and 12 of Schedule 5 and section 56(1) so far as relating to those paragraphs.

(8) Nothing in subsection (4) above affects the extent of this Act in so far as it—

(a) confers a power or imposes a duty on a court-martial or a Standing Civilian Court; or

(b) amends any provision of the Army Act 1955, the Air Force Act 1955 or the Naval Discipline Act 1957.

1955 c.18.
1955 c.19.
1957 c.53.

SCHEDULES

SCHEDULE 1

TRANSFER OF PRISONERS WITHIN THE BRITISH ISLANDS

PART I

POWERS OF TRANSFER

Transfer of prisoners: general

1.—(1) The Secretary of State may, on the application of—

   (a) a person remanded in custody in any part of the United Kingdom in connection with an offence; or

   (b) a person serving a sentence of imprisonment in any part of the United Kingdom,

make an order for his transfer to another part of the United Kingdom or to any of the Channel Islands, there to be remanded in custody pending his trial for the offence or, as the case may be, to serve the whole or any part of the remainder of his sentence, and for his removal to an appropriate institution there.

   (2) Where—

   (a) a person is remanded in custody in any of the Channel Islands in connection with an offence; or

   (b) a person has been sentenced to imprisonment in any of the Channel Islands,

the Secretary of State may, without application in that behalf, make an order for his transfer to any part of the United Kingdom, there to be remanded in custody pending his trial for the offence or, as the case may be, to serve the whole or any part of his sentence or the remainder of his sentence, and for his removal to an appropriate institution there.

   (3) In this paragraph "appropriate institution"—

   (a) in relation to a person remanded in custody, means any prison or other institution;

   (b) in relation to a person sentenced to imprisonment, means, subject to sub-paragraph (4) below, any institution which would be appropriate for the detention of an offender of the same age serving an equivalent sentence passed by a court in the country or island to which he is transferred.

   (4) Sub-paragraph (3)(b) above shall have effect in relation to a person serving a sentence of a length which could not have been passed on an offender of his age by a court in the place to which he has been transferred as if it defined "appropriate institution" as meaning such place as the Secretary of State may direct.

Transfer of prisoners for trial

2.—(1) If it appears to the Secretary of State that—

   (a) a person remanded in custody in any part of the United Kingdom in connection with an offence; or

   (b) a person serving a sentence of imprisonment in any part of the United Kingdom,

should be transferred to another part of the United Kingdom or to any of the Channel Islands for the purpose of attending criminal proceedings against him there, the Secretary of State may make an order for his transfer to that other part or that island and for his removal to a prison or other institution there.

(2) If it appears to the Secretary of State that—

> (a) a person remanded in custody in any of the Channel Islands in connection with an offence; or

> (b) a person serving a sentence of imprisonment in any of the Channel Islands,

should be transferred to a part of the United Kingdom for the purpose of attending criminal proceedings against him there, the Secretary of State may make an order for his transfer to that part and for his removal to a prison or other institution there.

(3) Where a person has been transferred under sub-paragraph (1)(a) or (2)(a) above for the purpose of any proceedings, the Secretary of State may, if that person is not sentenced to imprisonment in those proceedings, make an order for his return to the country or island from which he was transferred under that sub-paragraph.

(4) Where a person has been transferred under sub-paragraph (1)(b) or (2)(b) above for the purpose of any proceedings, the Secretary of State may—

> (a) if that person is sentenced to imprisonment in those proceedings, make an order under paragraph 1(1)(b) or (2)(b) above (but without application in that behalf) transferring him back to the country or island from which he was transferred under that sub-paragraph;

> (b) if he is not so sentenced, make an order for his return to the said country or island, there to serve the remainder of the sentence referred to in that sub-paragraph.

Transfer of prisoners for other judicial purposes

3.—(1) If the Secretary of State is satisfied, in the case of—

> (a) a person remanded in custody in any part of the United Kingdom in connection with an offence;

> (b) a person serving a sentence of imprisonment in any part of the United Kingdom; or

> (c) a person not falling within paragraph (a) or (b) above who is detained in a prison in any part of the United Kingdom,

that the attendance of that person at any place in that or any other part of the United Kingdom or in any of the Channel Islands is desirable in the interests of justice or for the purposes of any public inquiry, the Secretary of State may direct that person to be taken to that place.

(2) If the Secretary of State is satisfied, in the case of—

> (a) a person remanded in custody in any of the Channel Islands in connection with an offence;

> (b) a person serving a sentence of imprisonment in any of the Islands; or

> (c) a person not falling within paragraph (a) or (b) above who is detained in a prison in any of the Channel Islands,

that the attendance of that person at any place in the United Kingdom is desirable in the interests of justice or for the purposes of any public inquiry, the Secretary of State may direct that person to be taken to that place.

(3) Where any person is directed under this paragraph to be taken to any place he shall, unless the Secretary of State otherwise directs, be kept in custody while being so taken, while at that place, and while being taken back to the prison or other institution or place in which he is required in accordance with law to be detained.

Transfer of supervision of released prisoners

4.—(1) The Secretary of State may, on the application of a person undergoing or about to undergo supervision in any part of the United Kingdom, make an order for the transfer of his supervision to another part of the United Kingdom or to any of the Channel Islands, that is to say, an order—

(a) for his supervision or, as the case may be, the remainder of his supervision to be undergone in that country or island; and

(b) for responsibility for his supervision to be transferred to an appropriate person there.

(2) The Secretary of State may, on the application of a person undergoing or about to undergo supervision in any of the Channel Islands, make an order for the transfer of his supervision to any part of the United Kingdom, that is to say, an order—

(a) for his supervision or, as the case may be, the remainder of his supervision to be undergone in that country; and

(b) for responsibility for his supervision to be transferred to an appropriate person there.

Conditions of transfers

5.—(1) A transfer under this Part shall have effect subject to such conditions (if any) as the Secretary of State may think fit to impose.

(2) Subject to sub-paragraph (3) below, a condition imposed under this paragraph may be varied or removed at any time.

(3) Such a condition as is mentioned in paragraph 6(1)(a) below shall not be varied or removed except with the consent of the person to whom the transfer relates.

PART II

EFFECT OF TRANSFERS

Preliminary

6.—(1) For the purposes of this Part of this Schedule, a transfer under Part I of this Schedule—

(a) is a restricted transfer if it is subject to a condition that the person to whom it relates is to be treated for the relevant purposes as if he were still subject to the provisions applicable for those purposes under the law of the place from which the transfer is made; and

(b) is an unrestricted transfer if it is not so subject.

(2) In this Part of this Schedule "the relevant purposes" means—

(a) in relation to the transfer of a person under paragraph 1(1)(a) or (2)(a), 2(1)(a) or (2)(a) or 3(1)(a) or (2)(a) above, the purposes of his remand in custody and, where applicable, the purposes of his detention under and release from any sentence of imprisonment that may be imposed;

(b) in relation to the transfer of a person under paragraph 1(1)(b) or (2)(b), 2(1)(b) or (2)(b) or 3(1)(b) or (2)(b) above, the purposes of his detention under and release from his sentence and, where applicable, the purposes of his supervision and possible recall following his release; and

(c) in relation to the transfer of a person's supervision under paragraph 4(1) or (2) above, the purposes of his supervision and possible recall.

(3) In this paragraph "recall" means—

(a) in relation to a person who is supervised in pursuance of an order made for the purpose, being sentenced to imprisonment, or being recalled to prison, for a breach of any condition of the order;

(b) in relation to a person who is supervised in pursuance of a condition contained in a licence, being recalled to prison under the licence, whether for a breach of any condition of the licence or otherwise.

Restricted transfers: general

7.—(1) Where—

(a) a person's transfer under paragraph 1, 2 or 3 above; or

(b) a transfer under paragraph 4 above of a person's supervision,

is a restricted transfer, that person or, as the case may be, his supervision may by order be transferred back to the country or island from which he or it was transferred.

(2) Where a person's transfer under paragraph 1 or 2 above is a restricted transfer, that person shall while in the country or territory to which he is transferred be kept in custody except in so far as the Secretary of State may in any case or class of case otherwise direct.

Restricted transfers from England and Wales to Scotland

8.—(1) Where a person's transfer under paragraph 1(1)(a), 2(1)(a) or 3(1)(a) above from England and Wales to Scotland is a restricted transfer—

(a) regulations made under section 22 of the Prosecution of Offences Act 1985 (time limits in relation to preliminary stages of proceedings) shall apply to him in place of the corresponding provisions of the law of Scotland; but

(b) subject to that and to any conditions to which the transfer is subject, he shall be treated for the relevant purposes as if he had been remanded for an offence committed in Scotland.

1985 c.23.

(2) Where a person's transfer under paragraph 1(1)(b), 2(1)(b) or 3(1)(b) above from England and Wales to Scotland is a restricted transfer—

(a) sections 10, 12, 16, 17(1) to (4) and (6), 18(1) and (2), 19(1), (2), (6)(a) and (8) to (10), 20(1) and (2), 21(1) and (2), 23 and 27 of this Act or, as the case may require, sections 28 to 32 and 34 of this Act shall apply to him in place of the corresponding provisions of the law of Scotland; but

(b) subject to that, to sub-paragraph (3) below and to any conditions to which the transfer is subject, he shall be treated for the relevant purposes as if his sentence had been an equivalent sentence passed by a court in Scotland.

(3) A person who has been sentenced to a sentence of a length which could not have been passed on an offender of his age in the place to which he has been transferred shall be treated for the purposes mentioned in sub-paragraph (2) above as the Secretary of State may direct.

(4) Where a transfer under paragraph 4(1) above of a person's supervision from England and Wales to Scotland is a restricted transfer—

(a) sections 16, 17(1) to (4) and (6), 18(1) and (2), 19(1), (2), (6)(a) and (8) to (10), 20(1) and (2), 21(1) and (2) and 27 of this Act or, as the case may require, sections 31, 32 and 34 of this Act shall apply to him in place of the corresponding provisions of the law of Scotland; but

(b) subject to that and to any conditions to which the transfer is subject, he shall be treated for the relevant purposes as if his period of supervision had been an equivalent period of supervision directed to be undergone in Scotland.

SCH. 1

(5) Any provision of Part II of this Act which is applied by sub-paragraph (2) or (4) above shall have effect (as so applied) as if any reference to an expression specified in the first column of the following Table were a reference to the expression set out opposite it in the second column of that Table.

TABLE

Expression	Substituted expression
Crown Court	High Court of Justiciary
Information on oath	Evidence on oath
Magistrates' court	Sheriff
Probation officer	Relevant officer within the meaning given by section 27(1) of the Prisoners and Criminal Proceedings (Scotland) Act 1993

1993 c.9.

Restricted transfers from England and Wales to Northern Ireland

9.—(1) Where a person's transfer under paragraph 1(1)(a), 2(1)(a) or 3(1)(a) above from England and Wales to Northern Ireland is a restricted transfer—

(a) sections 13 and 15 of this Act shall apply to him as if they were part of the law of Northern Ireland; but

(b) subject to that and to any conditions to which the transfer is subject, he shall be treated for the relevant purposes as if he had been remanded for an offence committed in Northern Ireland.

(2) Where a person's transfer under paragraph 1(1)(b), 2(1)(b) or 3(1)(b) above from England and Wales to Northern Ireland is a restricted transfer—

(a) sections 10 to 12, 14, 16, 17(1), (2), (4) and (6), 18, 19(1), (2), (4), (6) and (8) to (10), 20(1) and (2), 21(1) and (2), 23 and 27 of this Act or, as the case may require, sections 28 to 32 and 34 of this Act shall apply to him in place of the corresponding provisions of the law of Northern Ireland; but

(b) subject to that, to sub-paragraph (3) below and to any conditions to which the transfer is subject, he shall be treated for the relevant purposes as if that sentence had been an equivalent sentence passed by a court in Northern Ireland.

(3) A person who has been sentenced to a sentence of a length which could not have been passed on an offender of his age in the place to which he has been transferred shall be treated for the purposes mentioned in sub-paragraph (2) above as the Secretary of State may direct.

(4) Where a transfer under paragraph 4(1) above of a person's supervision from England and Wales to Northern Ireland is a restricted transfer—

(a) sections 16, 17(1), (2), (4) and (6), 18, 19(1), (2), (6) and (8) to (10), 20(1) and (2), 21(1) and (2) and 27 of this Act or, as the case may require, sections 31, 32 and 34 of this Act shall apply to him in place of the corresponding provisions of the law of Northern Ireland; but

(b) subject to that and to any conditions to which the transfer is subject, he shall be treated for the relevant purposes as if his period of supervision had been an equivalent period of supervision directed to be undergone in Northern Ireland.

1952 c.52.

(5) In sub-paragraph (2) above, the reference to section 11 of this Act includes a reference to any rules under section 47 of the Prison Act 1952 which prescribe a minimum standard of behaviour for the purposes of the said section 11.

(6) Any provision of Part II of this Act which is applied by sub-paragraph (1), (2) or (4) above shall have effect (as so applied) as if any reference to an expression specified in the first column of the following Table were a reference to the expression set out opposite it in the second column of that Table.

TABLE

Expression	*Substituted expression*	
Community home	Training School	
Information on oath	Complaint on oath	
Prison rules	Rules made under section 13 of the Prison Act (Northern Ireland) 1953	1953 c.18 (N.I.).
Section 8 of the Police and Criminal Evidence Act 1984	Article 10 of the Police and Criminal Evidence (Northern Ireland) Order 1989	1984 c.60. S.I. 1989/1341 (N.I.12).
Social worker of a local authority social services department	Officer of a Board or an authorised Health and Social Services (HSS) Trust	

Restricted transfers from Scotland to England and Wales

10.—(1) Where a person's transfer under paragraph 1(1)(a), 2(1)(a) or 3(1)(a) above from Scotland to England and Wales is a restricted transfer—

    (a) sections 65 and 147 of the Criminal Procedure (Scotland) Act 1995 (time limits for solemn and summary prosecutions where prisoner remanded in custody) shall apply to him in the place of the corresponding provisions of the law of England and Wales; but   1995 c.46.

    (b) subject to that and to any conditions to which the transfer is subject, he shall be treated for the relevant purposes as if he had been remanded for an offence committed in England and Wales.

(2) Where a person's transfer under paragraph 1(1)(b), 2(1)(b) or 3(1)(b) from Scotland to England and Wales is a restricted transfer—

    (a) sections 15, 18 and 19 of the Prisoners and Criminal Proceedings (Scotland) Act 1993 ("the 1993 Act") and sections 33(5), 34, 37 and 39 of the Crime and Punishment (Scotland) Act 1997 ("the 1997 Act") or, as the case may require, sections 1(4), 2, 3, 11 to 13 and 17 of the 1993 Act shall apply to him in place of the corresponding provisions of the law of England and Wales; but   1993 c.9. 1997 c.48.

    (b) subject to that, to sub-paragraphs (3) and (4) below and to any conditions to which the transfer is subject, he shall be treated for the relevant purposes as if his sentence had been an equivalent sentence passed by a court in England and Wales.

(3) A person who has been sentenced to a sentence of a length which could not have been passed on an offender of his age in the place to which he is transferred shall be treated for the purposes mentioned in sub-paragraph (2) above as the Secretary of State may direct.

(4) Notwithstanding anything contained in sub-paragraph (2)(b) above, sections 16 to 18 of this Act shall not apply to a person whose transfer from Scotland to England and Wales is a restricted transfer.

(5) Where a transfer under paragraph 4(1) above of a person's supervision from Scotland to England and Wales is a restricted transfer—

    (a) sections 15, 18 and 19 of the 1993 Act and sections 33(5) and 37 of the 1997 Act or, as the case may require, sections 2(4), 11 to 13 and 17 of the 1993 Act shall apply to him in place of the corresponding provisions of the law of England and Wales; but

(b) subject to that and to any conditions to which the transfer is subject, he shall be treated for the relevant purposes as if his period of supervision had been an equivalent period of supervision directed to be undergone in England and Wales.

(6) Any reference in—

(a) sub-paragraphs (2) and (5) above to sections 15, 18 and 19 of the 1993 Act is a reference to those sections so far as relating to supervised release orders;

(b) in the said sub-paragraph (2)—

(i) to section 34 of the 1997 Act includes a reference to any rules under section 39 of the Prisons (Scotland) Act 1989 made by virtue of subsections (13) to (16) of that section; and

(ii) to section 39 of the 1997 Act is a reference to that section so far as it relates to section 37 of that Act.

(7) Any provision of Part I of the 1993 Act or Part III of the 1997 Act which is applied by sub-paragraph (2) or (5) above shall have effect (as so applied) as if any reference to an expression specified in the first column of the following Table were a reference to the expression set out opposite it in the second column of that Table.

TABLE

Expression	*Substituted expression*
Chief social work officer	Chief social worker of a local authority social services department
Young offenders institution	Young offender institution

Restricted transfers from Scotland to Northern Ireland

11.—(1) Where a person's transfer under paragraph 1(1)(a), 2(1)(a) or 3(1)(a) above from Scotland to Northern Ireland is a restricted transfer—

1995 c.46.

(a) sections 65 and 147 of the Criminal Procedure (Scotland) Act 1995 (time limits for solemn and summary prosecutions where prisoner remanded in custody) shall apply to him as if they were part of the law of Northern Ireland; but

(b) subject to that and to any conditions to which the transfer is subject, he shall be treated for the relevant purposes as if he had been remanded for an offence committed in Northern Ireland.

(2) Where a person's transfer under paragraph 1(1)(b), 2(1)(b) or 3(1)(b) from Scotland or Northern Ireland is a restricted transfer—

1993 c.9.

1997 c.48.

(a) sections 15, 18 and 19 of the Prisoners and Criminal Proceedings (Scotland) Act 1993 ("the 1993 Act") and sections 33(5), 34, 37 and 39 of the Crime and Punishment (Scotland) Act 1997 ("the 1997 Act") or, as the case may require, sections 1(4), 2, 3, 11 to 13 and 17 of the 1993 Act shall apply to him in place of the corresponding provisions of the law of Northern Ireland; but

(b) subject to that, to sub-paragraph (3) below and to any conditions to which the transfer is subject, he shall be treated for the relevant purposes as if his sentence had been an equivalent sentence passed by a court in Northern Ireland.

(3) A person who has been sentenced to a sentence of a length which could not have been passed on an offender of his age in the place to which he is transferred shall be treated for the purposes mentioned in sub-paragraph (2) above as the Secretary of State may direct.

(4) Where a transfer under paragraph 4(1) above of a person's supervision from Scotland to Northern Ireland is a restricted transfer—

(a) sections 15, 18 and 19 of the 1993 Act and sections 33(5) and 37 of the 1997 Act or, as the case may require, sections 2(4), 11 to 13 and 17 of the 1993 Act shall apply to him in place of the corresponding provisions of the law of Northern Ireland; but

(b) subject to that and to any conditions to which the transfer is subject, he shall be treated for the relevant purposes as if his period of supervision had been an equivalent period of supervision directed to be undergone in Northern Ireland.

(5) Sub-paragraph (5) of paragraph 10 above shall apply for the purposes of this paragraph as it applies for the purposes of that paragraph.

(6) Any provision of Part I of the 1993 Act or Part III of the 1997 Act which is applied by sub-paragraph (2) or (4) above shall have effect (as so applied) as if any reference to an expression specified in the first column of the following Table were a reference to the expression set out opposite it in the second column of that Table.

TABLE

Expression	Substituted expression
Chief social work officer	Chief Officer of a Board or an authorised Health and Social Services (HSS) Trust
Justices for a petty sessions area	Probation Board for Northern Ireland
Young offenders institution	Young offenders centre

Restricted transfers from Northern Ireland to England and Wales

12.—(1) Where a person's transfer under paragraph 1(1)(a), 2(1)(a) or 3(1)(a) above from Northern Ireland to England and Wales is a restricted transfer, subject to any conditions to which the transfer is subject, he shall be treated for the relevant purposes as if he had been remanded for an offence committed in England and Wales.

(2) Where a person's transfer under paragraph 1(1)(b), 2(1)(b) or 3(1)(b) above from Northern Ireland to England and Wales is a restricted transfer—

(a) sections 13(7), 23 and 24 of the Prison Act (Northern Ireland) 1953, Articles 3 to 6 of the Treatment of Offenders (Northern Ireland) Order 1976 and Articles 26 to 28 of the Criminal Justice (Northern Ireland) Order 1996 or, as the case may require, section 1 of the Northern Ireland (Remission of Sentences) Act 1995 shall apply to him in place of the corresponding provisions of the law of England and Wales; but

1953 c.18 (N.I.). S.I. 1976/226 (N.I.4). S.I. 1996/3160 (N.I.24). 1995 c.47.

(b) subject to that, to sub-paragraph (3) below and to any conditions to which the transfer is subject, he shall be treated for the relevant purposes as if that sentence had been an equivalent sentence passed by a court in England and Wales.

(3) A person who has been sentenced to a sentence of a length which could not have been passed on an offender of his age in the place to which he has been transferred shall be treated for the purposes mentioned in sub-paragraph (2) above as the Secretary of State may direct.

(4) Where a transfer under paragraph 4(1) of a person's supervision from Northern Ireland to England and Wales is a restricted transfer, subject to any conditions to which the transfer is subject, he shall be treated for the relevant purposes as if his period of supervision had been an equivalent period of supervision directed to be undergone in England and Wales.

Sch. 1
1953 c.18 (N.I.).
S.I. 1976/226
(N.I.4).
S.I. 1996/3160
(N.I.24).
1995 c.47.

(5) Any provision of the Prison Act (Northern Ireland) 1953, the Treatment of Offenders (Northern Ireland) Order 1976, the Criminal Justice (Northern Ireland) Order 1996 or the Northern Ireland (Remission of Sentences) Act 1995 which is applied by sub-paragraph (2) above shall have effect (as so applied) as if any reference to an expression specified in the first column of the following Table were a reference to the expression set out opposite it in the second column of that Table.

TABLE

Expression	Substituted Expression
Complaint on oath	Information on oath
Court of summary jurisdiction	Magistrates' court
Prison rules	Rules made under section 47 of the Prison Act 1952

Restricted transfers from Northern Ireland to Scotland

13.—(1) Where a person's transfer under paragraph 1(1)(a), 2(1)(a) or 3(1)(a) above from Northern Ireland to Scotland is a restricted transfer, subject to any conditions to which the transfer is subject, he shall be treated for the relevant purposes as if he had been remanded for an offence committed in Scotland.

(2) Where a person's transfer under paragraph 1(1)(b), 2(1)(b) or 3(1)(b) above from Northern Ireland to Scotland is a restricted transfer—

(a) sections 13(7), 23 and 24 of the Prison Act (Northern Ireland) 1953, Articles 3 to 6 of the Treatment of Offenders (Northern Ireland) Order 1976 and Articles 26 to 28 of the Criminal Justice (Northern Ireland) Order 1996 or, as the case may require, section 1 of the Northern Ireland (Remission of Sentences) Act 1995 shall apply to him in place of the corresponding provisions of the law of Scotland; but

S.I. 1996/3160
(N.I. 24).

(b) subject to that, to sub-paragraph (3) below and to any conditions to which the transfer is subject, he shall be treated for the relevant purposes as if that sentence had been an equivalent sentence passed by a court in Scotland.

(3) A person who has been sentenced to a sentence of a length which could not have been passed on an offender of his age in the place to which he has been transferred shall be treated for the purposes mentioned in sub-paragraph (2) above as the Secretary of State may direct.

(4) Where a transfer under paragraph 4(1) above of a person's supervision from Northern Ireland to Scotland is a restricted transfer, subject to any conditions to which the transfer is subject, he shall be treated for the relevant purposes as if his period of supervision had been an equivalent period of supervision directed to be undergone in Scotland.

(5) Any provision of the Prison Act (Northern Ireland) 1953, the Treatment of Offenders (Northern Ireland) Order 1976, the Criminal Justice (Northern Ireland) Order 1996 or the Northern Ireland (Remission of Sentences) Act 1995 which is applied by sub-paragraph (2) above shall have effect (as so applied) as if any reference to an expression specified in the first column of the following Table were a reference to the expression set out opposite it in the second column of that Table.

TABLE

Expression	Substituted Expression
Complaint on oath	Evidence on oath
Court of summary jurisdiction	Sheriff
Crown Court	High Court of Justiciary

Prison rules	Rules made under section 39 of the Prisons (Scotland) Act 1989	1989 c.45.
Probation officer	Relevant officer within the meaning of section 27(1) of the Prisoners and Criminal Proceedings (Scotland) Act 1993	1993 c.9.

Restricted transfers between the United Kingdom and the Channel Islands

14.—(1) Her Majesty may by Order in Council make, in relation to restricted transfers under Part I of this Schedule between any part of the United Kingdom and any of the Channel Islands, provision broadly corresponding to that made by any of paragraphs 8 to 13 above.

(2) An Order in Council under this paragraph may make such consequential, incidental, transitional and supplementary provision as Her Majesty considers appropriate.

(3) An Order in Council under this paragraph shall be subject to annulment in pursuance of a resolution of either House of Parliament.

Unrestricted transfers: general

15.—(1) Where a person's transfer under paragraph 1(1)(a) or (2)(a), 2(1)(a) or (2)(a) or 3(1)(a) or (2)(a) above to any part of the United Kingdom or to any of the Channel Islands is an unrestricted transfer, he shall be treated for the relevant purposes as if he had been remanded for an offence committed in the place to which he is transferred.

(2) Subject to sub-paragraph (3) below, where a person's transfer under paragraph 1(1)(b) or (2)(b), 2(1)(b) or (2)(b) or 3(1)(b) or (2)(b) above to any part of the United Kingdom or to any of the Channel Islands is an unrestricted transfer, he shall be treated for the relevant purposes as if his sentence had been an equivalent sentence passed by a court in the place to which he is transferred.

(3) A person who has been sentenced to a sentence of a length which could not have been passed on an offender of his age in the place to which he has been transferred shall be treated for the purposes mentioned in sub-paragraph (2) above as the Secretary of State may direct.

(4) Where a transfer under paragraph 4(1) or (2) above of a person's supervision to any part of the United Kingdom or to any of the Channel Islands is an unrestricted transfer—

(a) that person shall be treated for the relevant purposes as if his period of supervision had been an equivalent period of supervision directed to be undergone in the place to which he is transferred; and

(b) any functions of the Secretary of State under any provision of the law of that place which applies for those purposes shall be exercisable in relation to that person by any person appointed by the Secretary of State for the purpose.

(5) Where the relevant purposes in relation to a transfer to Scotland which is an unrestricted transfer include supervision, the person to whom the transfer relates shall be treated as if a supervised release order had been made in respect of him by such court as the Secretary of State may specify.

Transfers ceasing to be restricted

16. Where a transfer under Part I of this Schedule ceases to be a restricted transfer at any time by reason of the removal of such a condition as is mentioned in paragraph 6(1)(a) above, paragraph 15 above shall apply as if the transfer were an unrestricted transfer and had been effected at that time.

PART III

SUPPLEMENTAL

Prisoners unlawfully at large

17.—(1) The following enactments (relating to the arrest and return of prisoners and other persons unlawfully at large), namely—

1952 c.52.
(a) section 49(1) of the Prison Act 1952;

1989 c.45.
(b) section 40(1) of the Prisons (Scotland) Act 1989; and

1953 c.18 (N.I.).
(c) section 38(1) of the Prison Act (Northern Ireland) 1953,

shall extend throughout the United Kingdom and the Channel Islands.

(2) Any reference in those enactments to a constable shall include a reference—

(a) to a person being a constable under the law of any part of the United Kingdom;

(b) to a police officer within the meaning of the Police Force (Jersey) Law 1974 or any corresponding law for the time being in force; and

(c) to an officer of police within the meaning of section 31(4) of the Theft (Bailiwick of Guernsey) Law 1983 or any corresponding law for the time being in force.

(3) Those enactments shall also apply to persons who, being unlawfully at large under the law of any of the Channel Islands, are for the time being within the United Kingdom as they apply to persons unlawfully at large under the law of any part of the United Kingdom.

(4) Any person arrested in the United Kingdom under those enactments as applied by sub-paragraph (3) above may be taken to the place in the Channel Islands in which he is required in accordance with the law in force there to be detained.

(5) Where a person who, having been sentenced to imprisonment, is unlawfully at large during any period during which he is liable to be detained in a prison in any part of the United Kingdom is sentenced to imprisonment by a court in another part of the United Kingdom—

(a) the provisions of Part II of this Schedule relating to the treatment of persons transferred under sub-paragraph (1)(b) of paragraph 1 above shall apply to him, while he remains in that other part of the United Kingdom, as if he had been transferred there under that sub-paragraph immediately before he was so sentenced; and

(b) the Secretary of State may, if he thinks fit, make an order under that sub-paragraph (but without application in that behalf) transferring him back to the part of the United Kingdom from which he was unlawfully at large.

(6) In the following provisions, namely—

(a) paragraph (a) of the proviso to section 49(2) of the Prison Act 1952 (which in effect enables a person who is unlawfully at large during the currency of his original sentence to count towards that sentence any period during which he is detained in pursuance of a sentence of any court);

(b) the proviso to section 40(2) of the Prisons (Scotland) Act 1989 (which contains corresponding provisions for Scotland); and

(c) section 38(3) of the Prison Act (Northern Ireland) 1953 (which contains corresponding provisions for Northern Ireland),

references to a court shall include references to any court in the United Kingdom.

Subsequent sentence in case of transferred prisoners

18.—(1) The power of a court in any part of the United Kingdom to order that the term of any sentence of imprisonment passed by the court shall commence at or before the expiration of another term of imprisonment shall include power to make such an order where that other term was imposed by sentence of a court elsewhere in the United Kingdom or in any of the Channel Islands if the offender—

(a) is serving that other sentence in that part of the United Kingdom; or

(b) is for the time being present in that part of the United Kingdom,

by virtue of an order under this Schedule, or is unlawfully at large under the law of the country or island in which that other sentence was passed.

(2) The provisions of this paragraph shall be without prejudice to the powers exercisable by any court apart from those provisions.

Application to the Isle of Man

19.—(1) Her Majesty may by Order in Council direct that any of the foregoing provisions of this Schedule which extend to, or apply in relation to, the Channel Islands shall extend to, or apply in relation to, the Isle of Man with such modifications (if any) as Her Majesty considers appropriate.

(2) An Order in Council under this paragraph may make such consequential, incidental, transitional and supplementary provision as Her Majesty considers appropriate.

(3) An Order in Council under this paragraph shall be subject to annulment in pursuance of a resolution of either House of Parliament.

Interpretation

20.—(1) In this Schedule—

"prison", unless the context otherwise requires, includes a young offender institution, a young offenders institution, a young offenders centre and a remand centre;

"sentence of imprisonment" includes any sentence of detention and a sentence of custody for life under section 8 of the 1982 Act, and cognate expressions shall be construed accordingly;

"supervision" means supervision in pursuance of an order made for the purpose or, in the case of a person released from prison on licence, in pursuance of a condition contained in his licence.

(2) References in this Schedule to a person being remanded in custody are references to his being remanded in or committed to custody by an order of a court.

(3) In determining, in relation to any person serving a sentence of imprisonment, the time which is to be served in respect of an equivalent sentence treated as passed in another country or island, regard shall be had, not only to any time already served by him, but also to—

(a) any periods for which he has been remanded in custody, being either—

(i) periods by which his sentence falls to be reduced; or

(ii) periods which have been directed to count as time served as part of his sentence; and

(b) any early release or additional days awarded to him.

SCHEDULE 2

REPATRIATION OF PRISONERS TO THE BRITISH ISLANDS

Preliminary

1. Any reference in this Schedule to prisoners repatriated to any part of the United Kingdom is a reference to prisoners transferred there in pursuance of a warrant issued under the Repatriation of Prisoners Act 1984 ("the 1984 Act").

Prisoners repatriated to England and Wales

2.—(1) This paragraph applies in relation to—

(a) prisoners repatriated to England and Wales before 25th October 1996 who were still serving their sentences on that date; and

(b) prisoners repatriated to England and Wales on or after that date and before the commencement of this Schedule.

(2) Paragraph 2 of the Schedule to the 1984 Act shall have effect, and shall be deemed always to have had effect, with the omission of sub-paragraph (1A) and the insertion after sub-paragraph (2) of the following sub-paragraphs—

"(3) The following questions, namely—

(a) whether the prisoner is a short-term or long-term prisoner for the purposes of the enactments relating to release on licence; and

(b) whether or not he is an existing prisoner for the purposes of paragraph 8 of Schedule 12 to the 1991 Act,

shall be determined by reference to the length or, as the case may require, commencement of the sentence imposed in the country or territory from which he is transferred.

(4) In this paragraph—

"the enactments relating to release on licence" means sections 33(1)(b) and (2), 34(3) and (5), 35(1) and 37(1) and (2) of the Criminal Justice Act 1991;

"sentence", except in sub-paragraph (3) above, means the provision included in the warrant which is equivalent to a sentence."

3.—(1) This paragraph applies in relation to prisoners repatriated to England and Wales after the commencement of this Schedule whose sentences in the country or territory from which they are transferred were imposed for offences committed before the commencement of Chapter I of Part II of this Act.

(2) In paragraph 2 of the Schedule to the 1984 Act, for sub-paragraphs (1A) and (2) there shall be substituted the following sub-paragraphs—

"(2) If the warrant specifies a period to be taken into account for the purposes of sections 34(3) and (5) and 35(1) of the Criminal Justice Act 1991—

(a) the amount of time the prisoner has served; and

(b) where his sentence is a determinate one, his sentence,

shall, so far only as the question whether he has served any particular proportion or part of his sentence is concerned, be deemed to be increased by that period.

(3) The following questions, namely—

(a) whether the prisoner is a long-term prisoner for the purposes of the enactments relating to release on licence; and

(b) whether or not he is an existing prisoner for the purposes of paragraph 8 of Schedule 12 to the 1991 Act,

shall be determined by reference to the length or, as the case may require, commencement of the sentence imposed in the country or territory from which he is transferred.

(4) In this paragraph—

"the enactments relating to release on licence" means sections 33(1)(b) and (2), 34(3) and (5), 35(1) and 37(1) and (2) of the Criminal Justice Act 1991;   1991 c.53.

"sentence", except in sub-paragraph (3) above, means the provision included in the warrant which is equivalent to a sentence."

4.—(1) This paragraph applies in relation to prisoners repatriated to England and Wales after the commencement of this Schedule whose sentences in the country or territory from which they are transferred were imposed for offences committed after the commencement of Chapter I of Part II of this Act.

(2) In section 2 of the 1984 Act (transfer of prisoners out of United Kingdom), in subsection (4)(b), for sub-paragraph (i) there shall be substituted the following sub-paragraph—

"(i) subject to a release supervision order under section 16 of the Crime (Sentences) Act 1997, or released on licence under section 28(5) or 29(1) of that Act;".

(3) In section 3 of the 1984 Act (transfer of prisoners into United Kingdom), in subsection (9)—

(a) for the words "section 48 of the Criminal Justice Act 1991 (discretionary life prisoners transferred to England and Wales)" there shall be substituted the words "section 33 of the Crime (Sentences) Act 1997 (life prisoner transferred to England and Wales)"; and

(b) for the words "section 34 of that Act (duty of Secretary of State to release discretionary life prisoners)" there shall be substituted the words "section 28 of that Act (duty to release certain life prisoners)".

(4) For paragraph 2 of the Schedule to the 1984 Act there shall be substituted the following paragraph—

"Early release

2.—(1) Subject to sub-paragraph (2) below, the prisoner's sentence, that is to say, the provision included in the warrant which is equivalent to a sentence, shall be deemed—

(a) for the purposes of Chapter I of Part II of the Crime (Sentences) Act 1997, to have been imposed on the day on which the relevant provisions take effect;

(b) for the purposes of Chapter II of that Part, to have been imposed on the same day as the sentence imposed in the country or territory from which he is transferred.

(2) The question whether—

(a) section 11 of the Crime (Sentences) Act 1997 (award of early release days for good behaviour); or

(b) section 12 of that Act (release on Parole Board recommendation),

applies in the case of the prisoner shall be determined by reference to the length of the sentence imposed in the country or territory from which he is transferred."

(5) For paragraph 3 of that Schedule there shall be substituted the following paragraph—

"Life imprisonment

3. Where the relevant provisions include provision equivalent to a sentence in relation to which subsection (1) of section 29 of the Crime (Sentences) Act 1997 (power to release certain life prisoners etc.) applies, that subsection shall have effect as if the reference to consultation with the trial judge if available were omitted."

Prisoners repatriated to Scotland

5.—(1) This paragraph applies in relation to—

(a) prisoners repatriated to Scotland before 25th October 1996 (the "relevant date") who were still serving sentences, which were imposed before 1st October 1993 in the country or territory from which they were transferred, on the relevant date; and

(b) prisoners repatriated to Scotland in respect of such sentences on or after the relevant date.

(2) Paragraph 2 of the Schedule to the 1984 Act, as originally enacted, shall have effect, and shall be deemed to have had effect since 16th February 1990, as if—

(a) in sub-paragraph (1), for the words "section 60 of the Criminal Justice Act 1967" there were substituted the words "section 22 of the Prisons (Scotland) Act 1989"; and

(b) at the end there were added the following sub-paragraph—

"(3) In this paragraph "sentence" means the provision included in a warrant which is equivalent to a sentence."

6.—(1) This paragraph applies in relation to—

(a) prisoners repatriated to Scotland before 25th October 1996 (the "relevant date") who were still serving sentences, which were imposed on or after 1st October 1993 in the country or territory from which they were transferred, on the relevant date; and

(b) prisoners repatriated to Scotland in respect of such sentences on or after the relevant date and before the commencement of this Schedule.

(2) Paragraph 2 of the Schedule to the 1984 Act shall have effect, and shall be deemed always to have had effect, with the omission of sub-paragraph (1A) and the insertion after sub-paragraph (2) of the following sub-paragraphs—

"(3) The question whether the prisoner is a short-term or long-term prisoner for the purposes of the enactments relating to release on licence shall be determined by reference to the length of the sentence imposed in the country or territory from which he is transferred.

1993 c.9.

(4) For the purposes of Schedule 6 to the Prisoners and Criminal Proceedings (Scotland) Act 1993 a prisoner's sentence shall be deemed to have been imposed on the day on which the relevant provisions take effect.

(5) In this paragraph—

"the enactments relating to release on licence" means sections 1(2) and (3), 2(2) and (7) and 7(1) of the Prisoners and Criminal Proceedings (Scotland) Act 1993;

"sentence", except in sub-paragraph (3) above, means the provision included in the warrant which is equivalent to a sentence."

7.—(1) This paragraph applies in relation to prisoners repatriated to Scotland after the commencement of this Schedule whose sentences in the country or territory from which they are transferred were imposed on or after 1st October 1993 for offences committed before the commencement of section 33 of the Crime and Punishment (Scotland) Act 1997.

(2) In paragraph 2 of the Schedule to the 1984 Act, for sub-paragraphs (1A) and (2) there shall be substituted the following sub-paragraphs—

"(2) If the warrant specifies a period to be taken into account for the purposes of sections 1(3) and 2(2) and (7) of the Prisoners and Criminal Proceedings (Scotland) Act 1993—

(a) the amount of time the prisoner has served; and

(b) where his sentence is a determinate one, his sentence,

shall, so far only as the question whether he has served any particular proportion or part of his sentence is concerned, be deemed to be increased by that period.

(3) The question whether the prisoner is a long-term prisoner for the purposes of the enactments relating to release on licence shall be determined by reference to the length of the sentence imposed in the country or territory from which he is transferred.

(4) For the purposes of Schedule 6 to the Prisoners and Criminal Proceedings (Scotland) Act 1993 a prisoner's sentence shall be deemed to have been imposed on the day on which the relevant provisions take effect.

(5) In this paragraph—

"the enactments relating to release on licence" means sections 1(2) and (3), 2(2) and (7) and 7(1) of the Prisoners and Criminal Proceedings (Scotland) Act 1993;

"sentence", except in sub-paragraph (3) above, means the provision included in the warrant which is equivalent to a sentence."

8.—(1) This paragraph applies in relation to prisoners repatriated to Scotland after the commencement of this Schedule whose sentences in the country or territory from which they are transferred were imposed for offences committed after the commencement of section 33 of the Crime and Punishment (Scotland) Act 1997.

(2) For paragraph 2 of the Schedule to the 1984 Act there shall be substituted the following paragraph—

"Early release

2. The prisoner's sentence, that is to say, the provision included in the warrant which is equivalent to a sentence, shall be deemed—

(a) for the purposes of Chapter I of Part III of the Crime and Punishment (Scotland) Act 1997, to have been imposed on the day on which the relevant provisions take effect;

(b) for the purposes of section 2(2) and (7) of the Prisoners and Criminal Proceedings (Scotland) Act 1993, to have been imposed on the same day as the sentence imposed in the country or territory from which he is transferred."

(3) For paragraph 3 of that Schedule there shall be substituted the following paragraph—

"Life imprisonment

3. Where the relevant provisions include provision equivalent to a sentence in relation to which subsection (4) of section 1 of the Prisoners and Criminal Proceedings (Scotland) Act 1993 (power to release certain life prisoners etc.) applies, that subsection shall have effect as if the reference to consultation with the trial judge if available were omitted."

Prisoners repatriated to Northern Ireland

9.—(1) This paragraph applies in relation to—

(a) prisoners repatriated to Northern Ireland before 25th October 1996 who were still serving their sentences on that date; and

(b) prisoners repatriated to Northern Ireland on or after that date.

(2) Paragraph 2 of the Schedule to the 1984 Act shall have effect, and shall be deemed always to have had effect, with the insertion after sub-paragraph (2) of the following sub-paragraph—

"(3) In this paragraph "sentence" means the provision included in the warrant which is equivalent to a sentence."

10.—(1) This paragraph applies in relation to prisoners repatriated to Northern Ireland after the commencement of this Schedule.

(2) For paragraph 3 of the Schedule to the 1984 Act there shall be substituted the following paragraph—

"Life imprisonment

3. Where the relevant provisions include provision equivalent to a sentence in relation to which subsection (3) of section 1 of the Northern Ireland (Emergency Provisions) Act 1973 (power to release certain life prisoners etc.) applies, that subsection shall have effect as if the reference to consultation with the trial judge if available were omitted."

Prisoners repatriated to the Islands

11.—(1) This paragraph applies where any Order in Council under section 9(4) of the 1984 Act extends the provisions of that Act to any of the Channel Islands or the Isle of Man.

(2) The modifications of that Act made by the Order may include modifications broadly corresponding to those made by any of paragraphs 1 to 10 above.

Section 48.

SCHEDULE 3

TRANSFERS WITHIN THE BRITISH ISLANDS OF RESPONSIBILITY FOR OFFENDERS CONDITIONALLY DISCHARGED FROM HOSPITAL

PART I

AMENDMENTS OF THE 1983 ACT

Transfers from England and Wales to Scotland

1. After section 80 of the 1983 Act there shall be inserted the following section—

"Transfer of responsibility for patients to Scotland.

80A.—(1) If it appears to the Secretary of State, in the case of a patient who—

(a) is subject to a restriction order under section 41 above; and

(b) has been conditionally discharged under section 42 or 73 above,

that a transfer under this section would be in the interests of the patient, the Secretary of State may, with the consent of the Minister exercising corresponding functions in Scotland, transfer responsibility for the patient to that Minister.

(2) Where responsibility for such a patient is transferred under this section, the patient shall be treated—

    (a) as if on the date of the transfer he had been conditionally discharged under the corresponding enactment in force in Scotland; and

    (b) as if he were subject to a restriction order under the corresponding enactment in force in Scotland.

(3) Where a patient responsibility for whom is transferred under this section was immediately before the transfer subject to a restriction order of limited duration, the restriction order to which he is subject by virtue of subsection (2) above shall expire on the date on which the first-mentioned order would have expired if the transfer had not been made."

Transfers from England and Wales to Northern Ireland

2. After section 81 of the 1983 Act there shall be inserted the following section—

"Transfer of responsibility for patients to Northern Ireland.

81A.—(1) If it appears to the Secretary of State, in the case of a patient who—

    (a) is subject to a restriction order or restriction direction under section 41 or 49 above; and

    (b) has been conditionally discharged under section 42 or 73 above,

that a transfer under this section would be in the interests of the patient, the Secretary of State may, with the consent of the Minister exercising corresponding functions in Northern Ireland, transfer responsibility for the patient to that Minister.

(2) Where responsibility for such a patient is transferred under this section, the patient shall be treated—

    (a) as if on the date of the transfer he had been conditionally discharged under the corresponding enactment in force in Northern Ireland; and

    (b) as if he were subject to a restriction order or restriction direction under the corresponding enactment in force in Northern Ireland.

(3) Where a patient responsibility for whom is transferred under this section was immediately before the transfer subject to a restriction order or restriction direction of limited duration, the restriction order or restriction direction to which he is subject by virtue of subsection (2) above shall expire on the date on which the first-mentioned order or direction would have expired if the transfer had not been made."

Transfers from Northern Ireland to England and Wales

3. After section 82 of the 1983 Act there shall be inserted the following section—

"Transfer of responsibility for patients to England and Wales from Northern Ireland.

82A.—(1) If it appears to the relevant Minister, in the case of a patient who—

    (a) is subject to a restriction order or restriction direction under Article 47(1) or 55(1) of the Mental Health (Northern Ireland) Order 1986; and

    (b) has been conditionally discharged under Article 48(2)

S.I. 1986/596 (N.I.4).

or 78(2) of that Order,

that a transfer under this section would be in the interests of the patient, that Minister may, with the consent of the Secretary of State, transfer responsibility for the patient to the Secretary of State.

(2) Where responsibility for such a patient is transferred under this section, the patient shall be treated—

    (a) as if on the date of the transfer he had been conditionally discharged under section 42 or 73 above; and

    (b) as if he were subject to a restriction order or restriction direction under section 41 or 49 above.

(3) Where a patient responsibility for whom is transferred under this section was immediately before the transfer subject to a restriction order or restriction direction of limited duration, the restriction order or restriction direction to which he is subject by virtue of subsection (2) above shall expire on the date on which the first-mentioned order or direction would have expired if the transfer had not been made.

(4) In this section 'the relevant Minister' means the Minister exercising in Northern Ireland functions corresponding to those of the Secretary of State."

Transfers from England and Wales to the Islands

4. After section 83 of the 1983 Act there shall be inserted the following section—

"Transfer of responsibility for patients to Channel Islands or Isle of Man.

    83A. If it appears to the Secretary of State, in the case of a patient who—

    (a) is subject to a restriction order or restriction direction under section 41 or 49 above; and

    (b) has been conditionally discharged under section 42 or 73 above,

that a transfer under this section would be in the interests of the patient, the Secretary of State may, with the consent of the authority exercising corresponding functions in any of the Channel Islands or in the Isle of Man, transfer responsibility for the patient to that authority."

Transfers from the Islands to England and Wales

5. After section 85 of the 1983 Act there shall be inserted the following section—

"Responsibility for patients transferred from Channel Islands or Isle of Man.

    85A.—(1) This section applies to any patient responsibility for whom is transferred to the Secretary of State by the authority exercising corresponding functions in any of the Channel Islands or the Isle of Man under a provision corresponding to section 83A above.

(2) The patient shall be treated—

    (a) as if on the date of the transfer he had been conditionally discharged under section 42 or 73 above; and

    (b) as if he were subject to a restriction order or restriction direction under section 41 or 49 above.

(3) Where the patient was immediately before the transfer subject to an order or direction restricting his discharge, being an order or direction of limited duration, the restriction order or restriction direction to which he is subject by virtue of subsection (2) above shall expire on the date on which the first-mentioned order or direction would have expired if the transfer had not been made."

Part II

Amendments of the 1984 Act

Transfers from Scotland to England and Wales

6. After section 77 of the 1984 Act there shall be inserted the following section—

"Transfer of responsibility for patients to England and Wales.

77A.—(1) If it appears to the Secretary of State, in the case of a patient who—

    (a) is subject to a restriction order under section 59 of the Criminal Procedure (Scotland) Act 1995; and

    (b) has been conditionally discharged under section 64 or 68 of this Act,

1995 c.46.

that a transfer under this section would be in the interests of the patient, the Secretary of State may, with the consent of the Minister exercising corresponding functions in England and Wales, transfer responsibility for the patient to that Minister.

(2) Where responsibility for such a patient is transferred under this section, the patient shall be treated—

    (a) as if on the date of the transfer he had been conditionally discharged under the corresponding enactment in force in England and Wales; and

    (b) as if he were subject to a restriction order under the corresponding enactment in force in England and Wales."

Transfers from Scotland to Northern Ireland

7. After section 80 of the 1984 Act there shall be inserted the following section—

"Transfer of responsibility for patients to Northern Ireland.

80A.—(1) If it appears to the Secretary of State, in the case of a patient who—

    (a) is subject to a restriction order under section 59 of the Criminal Procedure (Scotland) Act 1995; and

    (b) has been conditionally discharged under section 64 or 68 of this Act,

that a transfer under this section would be in the interests of the patient, the Secretary of State may, with the consent of the Minister exercising corresponding functions in Northern Ireland, transfer responsibility for the patient to that Minister.

(2) Where responsibility for such a patient is transferred under this section, the patient shall be treated—

    (a) as if on the date of the transfer he had been conditionally discharged under the corresponding enactment in force in Northern Ireland; and

    (b) as if he were subject to a restriction order under the corresponding enactment in force in Northern Ireland."

SCH. 3

Transfers from Northern Ireland to Scotland

8. After section 81 of the 1984 Act there shall be inserted the following section—

"Transfer of responsibility for patients to Scotland from Northern Ireland.

S.I. 1986/596 (N.I.4).

81A.—(1) If it appears to the relevant Minister, in the case of a patient who—

   (a) is subject to a restriction order under Article 47(1) of the Mental Health (Northern Ireland) Order 1986; and

   (b) has been conditionally discharged under Article 48(2) or 78(2) of that Order,

that a transfer under this section would be in the interests of the patient, that Minister may, with the consent of the Secretary of State, transfer responsibility for the patient to the Secretary of State.

(2) Where responsibility for such a patient is transferred under this section, the patient shall be treated—

   (a) as if on the date of the transfer he had been conditionally discharged under section 64 or 68 of this Act; and

   (b) as if he were subject to a restriction order within the meaning of this Act.

(3) Where a patient responsibility for whom is transferred under this section was immediately before the transfer subject to a restriction order of limited duration, the restriction order to which he is subject by virtue of subsection (2) above shall expire on the date on which the first-mentioned order would have expired if the transfer had not been made.

(4) In this section 'the relevant Minister' means the Minister exercising in Northern Ireland functions corresponding to those of the Secretary of State."

Transfers from the Islands to Scotland

9. After section 82 of the 1984 Act there shall be inserted the following section—

"Responsibility for patients transferred from Channel Islands or Isle of Man to Scotland.

82A.—(1) This section applies to any patient responsibility for whom is transferred to the Secretary of State by the authority exercising corresponding functions in any of the Channel Islands or the Isle of Man under a provision corresponding to section 82B of this Act.

(2) The patient shall be treated—

   (a) as if on the date of the transfer he had been conditionally discharged under section 64 or 68 of this Act; and

   (b) as if he were subject to a restriction order within the meaning of this Act.

(3) Where the patient was immediately before the transfer subject to an order restricting his discharge, being an order of limited duration, the restriction order to which he is subject by virtue of subsection (2) above shall expire on the date on which the first-mentioned order would have expired if the transfer had not been made."

Transfers from Scotland to the Islands

10. After section 82A of the 1984 Act there shall be inserted the following section—

"Transfer of
responsibility for
patients to
Channel Islands
or Isle of Man.

82B. If it appears to the Secretary of State, in the case of a patient who—

(a) is subject to a restriction order under section 59 of the Criminal Procedure (Scotland) Act 1995; and   1995 c.46.

(b) has been conditionally discharged under section 64 or 68 of this Act,

that a transfer under this section would be in the interests of the patient, the Secretary of State may, with the consent of the authority exercising corresponding functions in any of the Channel Islands or in the Isle of Man, transfer responsibility for the patient to that authority."

SCHEDULE 4

Section 55.

MINOR AND CONSEQUENTIAL AMENDMENTS

Army Act 1955 (c.18)

1.—(1) After subsection (3) of section 70 of the Army Act 1955 (civil offences) there shall be inserted the following subsection—

"(3A) Where the corresponding civil offence is one to which section 2, 3 or 4 of the Crime (Sentences) Act 1997 would apply, the court-martial shall impose the sentence required by subsection (2) of that section unless it is of the opinion that there are exceptional circumstances which justify its not doing so."

(2) For subsection (1A) of section 71A of that Act (juveniles) there shall be substituted the following subsection—

"(1A) Where—

(a) a person under 21 years of age is convicted of murder or any other civil offence the sentence for which is fixed by law as imprisonment for life; or

(b) a person under that age is convicted of any civil offence to which section 2 of the Crime (Sentences) Act 1997 would apply and the court is not of the opinion mentioned in subsection (2) of that section,

the court shall sentence him to custody for life unless he is liable to be detained under subsection (3) below."

(3) In subsection (6A) of section 71AA of that Act (young service offenders: custodial orders), for the words "Section 65 of the Criminal Justice Act 1991" there shall be substituted the words "Sections 16 and 17 of the Crime (Sentences) Act 1997 (as modified by section 19 of that Act)".

(4) In paragraph 3(1) of Schedule 5A to that Act (powers of court on trial of civilian), after the words "fixed by law" there shall be inserted the words "or falls to be imposed under section 70(3A) above".

(5) In paragraph 10(6A) of that Schedule, for the words "Section 65 of the Criminal Justice Act 1991" there shall be substituted the words "Sections 16 and 17 of the Crime (Sentences) Act 1997 (as modified by section 19 of that Act)".

Air Force Act 1955 (c.19)

2.—(1) After subsection (3) of section 70 of the Air Force Act 1955 (civil offences) there shall be inserted the following subsection—

"(3A) Where the corresponding civil offence is one to which section 2, 3 or 4 of the Crime (Sentences) Act 1997 would apply, the court-martial shall impose the sentence required by subsection (2) of that section unless it is of the opinion that there are exceptional circumstances which justify its not doing so."

(2) For subsection (1A) of section 71A of that Act (juveniles) there shall be substituted the following subsection—

"(1A) Where—

(a) a person under 21 years of age is convicted of murder or any other civil offence the sentence for which is fixed by law as imprisonment for life; or

(b) a person under that age is convicted of any civil offence to which section 2 of the Crime (Sentences) Act 1997 would apply and the court is not of the opinion mentioned in subsection (2) of that section,

the court shall sentence him to custody for life unless he is liable to be detained under subsection (3) below."

(3) In subsection (6A) of section 71AA of that Act (young service offenders: custodial orders), for the words "Section 65 of the Criminal Justice Act 1991" there shall be substituted the words "Sections 16 and 17 of the Crime (Sentences) Act 1997 (as modified by section 19 of that Act)".

(4) In paragraph 3(1) of Schedule 5A to that Act (powers of court on trial of civilian), after the words "fixed by law" there shall be inserted the words "or falls to be imposed under section 70(3A) above".

(5) In paragraph 10(6A) of that Schedule, for the words "Section 65 of the Criminal Justice Act 1991" there shall be substituted the words "Sections 16 and 17 of the Crime (Sentences) Act 1997 (as modified by section 19 of that Act)".

Naval Discipline Act 1957 (c.53)

3.—(1) After subsection (1) of section 42 of the Naval Discipline Act 1957 (civil offences) there shall be inserted the following subsection—

"(1A) Where the corresponding civil offence is one to which section 2, 3 or 4 of the Crime (Sentences) Act 1997 would apply, the court-martial shall impose the sentence required by subsection (2) of that section unless it is of the opinion that there are exceptional circumstances which justify its not doing so."

(2) For subsection (1A) of section 43A of that Act (juveniles) there shall be substituted the following subsection—

"(1A) Where—

(a) a person under 21 years of age is convicted of murder or any other civil offence the sentence for which is fixed by law as imprisonment for life; or

(b) a person under that age is convicted of any civil offence to which section 2 of the Crime (Sentences) Act 1997 would apply and the court is not of the opinion mentioned in subsection (2) of that section,

the court shall sentence him to custody for life unless he is liable to be detained under subsection (3) below."

(3) In subsection (6A) of section 43AA of that Act (young service offenders: custodial orders), for the words "Section 65 of the Criminal Justice Act 1991" there shall be substituted the words "Sections 16 and 17 of the Crime (Sentences) Act 1997 (as modified by section 19 of that Act)".

(4) In paragraph 3(1) of Schedule 4A to that Act (powers of court on trial of civilian), after the words "fixed by law" there shall be inserted the words "or falls to be imposed under section 42(1A) above".

(5) In paragraph 10(6A) of that Schedule, for the words "Section 65 of the Criminal Justice Act 1991" there shall be substituted the words "Sections 16 and 17 of the Crime (Sentences) Act 1997 (as modified by section 19 of that Act)".

Children and Young Persons Act 1963 (c.37)

4. After subsection (2) of section 16 of the Children and Young Persons Act 1963 (offences committed by children under 14 to be disregarded for purposes of evidence relating to previous convictions) there shall be inserted the following subsection—

"(3) Nothing in subsection (2) of this section shall be taken to prevent the adduction of evidence of previous convictions for the purpose of establishing the application of any provision of Part I of the Crime (Sentences) Act 1997 (mandatory and minimum custodial sentences)."

Criminal Justice Act 1967 (c.80)

5.—(1) In subsection (2) of section 56 of the Criminal Justice Act 1967 (committal for sentence for offences tried summarily)—

(a) for the words "sections 37 and 38" there shall be substituted the words "sections 37, 38 and 38A"; and

(b) for the words "and section 62(6) of this Act" there shall be substituted the words ", section 17(3) of the Crime (Sentences) Act 1997 (committal for breach of conditions of release supervision order),".

(2) In subsection (4) of section 72 of that Act (power of magistrates to issue warrants for escaped prisoners and mental patients), after the words "restricting his discharge" there shall be inserted the words "or in pursuance of a hospital direction and a limitation direction".

Criminal Appeal Act 1968 (c.19)

6.—(1) In subsection (1) of section 50 of the Criminal Appeal Act 1968 (meaning of sentence)—

(a) after paragraph (b) there shall be inserted the following paragraph—

"(bb) a hospital direction and a limitation direction under that Part;"; and

(b) after paragraph (c) there shall be inserted the following paragraph—

"(cc) a direction under section 20(3) or 21(3) of the Crime (Sentences) Act 1997 (extended supervision for sexual or violent offenders);".

(2) In sub-paragraph (4) of paragraph 2 of Schedule 2 to that Act (procedural and other provisions applicable on order for retrial), for the words "Section 67 of the Criminal Justice Act 1967 (deduction from certain sentences of time spent in custody before sentence)" there shall be substituted the words "Section 9 of the Crime (Sentences) Act 1997 (crediting of periods of remand in custody)".

Immigration Act 1971 (c.77)

7. In subsection (4) of section 7 of the Immigration Act 1971 (exemption from deportation for certain existing residents), for the words "section 67 of the Criminal Justice Act 1967" there shall be substituted the words "section 9 of the Crime (Sentences) Act 1997".

Powers of Criminal Courts Act 1973 (c.62)

8.—(1) In section 1A(1) of the 1973 Act (absolute and conditional discharge), after the words "is fixed by law" there shall be inserted the words "or falls to be imposed under section 2(2), 3(2) or 4(2) of the Crime (Sentences) Act 1997".

(2) In section 2(1) of that Act (probation orders), after the words "is fixed by law" there shall be inserted the words "or falls to be imposed under section 2(2), 3(2) or 4(2) of the Crime (Sentences) Act 1997".

(3) In section 30(1) of that Act (general power to fine offender), after the words "is fixed by law" there shall be inserted the words "or falls to be imposed under section 2(2), 3(2) or 4(2) of the Crime (Sentences) Act 1997".

(4) In subsection (1) of section 42 of that Act (power of Crown Court on committal for sentence), after the words "section 38" there shall be inserted the words "or 38A".

Rehabilitation of Offenders Act 1974 (c.53)

9.—(1) In subsection (2) of section 1 of the Rehabilitation of Offenders Act 1974 (rehabilitated persons and spent convictions), after paragraph (c) there shall be inserted the following paragraph—

> "(d) breach of any condition of a release supervision order made under section 16 of the Crime (Sentences) Act 1997."

(2) In subsection (6) of section 6 of that Act (the rehabilitation period applicable to a conviction), at the end of paragraph (a) there shall be inserted the words "or of an offence under section 17 of the Crime (Sentences) Act 1997 (breach of conditions of release supervision order)".

Magistrates' Courts Act 1980 (c.43)

10.—(1) In subsection (4A) of section 82 of the 1980 Act (restriction on power to impose imprisonment for default), in paragraph (e) for the words "under the age of 21" there shall be substituted the words "under the age of 25".

(2) For subsection (3) of section 85 of that Act (power to remit fine) there shall be substituted the following subsections—

> "(2A) Where the court remits the whole or part of the fine after an order has been made under section 35(2)(a) or (b) of the Crime (Sentences) Act 1997, it shall also reduce the total number of hours or days to which the order relates by a number which bears the same proportion as the amount remitted bears to the whole sum or, as the case may be, shall revoke the order.
>
> (3) In calculating any reduction required by subsection (2) or (2A) above any fraction of a day or hour shall be left out of account."

Criminal Justice Act 1982 (c.48)

11. In subsection (4) of section 1A of the 1982 Act (detention in a young offender institution), for the words "section 65(6) of the Criminal Justice Act 1991" there shall be substituted the words "section 17(1) of the Crime (Sentences) Act 1997 as it has effect by virtue of section 19 of that Act".

Mental Health Act 1983 (c.20)

12.—(1) In subsection (1) of section 37 of the 1983 Act (powers of courts to order hospital admission or guardianship), after the words "is fixed by law" there shall be inserted the words "or falls to be imposed under section 2(2) of the Crime Sentences) Act 1997".

(2) After that subsection there shall be inserted the following subsection—

"(1A) In the case of an offence the sentence for which would otherwise fall to be imposed under subsection (2) of section 3 or 4 of the Crime (Sentences) Act 1997, nothing in that subsection shall prevent a court from making an order under subsection (1) above for the admission of the offender to a hospital."

(3) In subsection (4) of that section, the words "in the event of such an order being made by the court" shall cease to have effect.

(4) After subsection (3) of section 50 of that Act (further provisions as to prisoners under sentence) there shall be inserted the following subsection—

"(3A) In applying subsection (3) above account shall be taken of any early release days awarded to the person under section 11 of the Crime (Sentences) Act 1997 (read with section 22 of that Act)."

(5) After subsection (4) of that section there shall be inserted the following subsection—

"(5) The preceding provisions of this section shall have effect as if—

(a) the reference in subsection (1) to a transfer direction and a restriction direction having been given in respect of a person serving a sentence of imprisonment included a reference to a hospital direction and a limitation direction having been given in respect of a person sentenced to imprisonment;

(b) the reference in subsection (2) to a restriction direction included a reference to a limitation direction; and

(c) references in subsections (3) and (4) to a transfer direction included references to a hospital direction."

(6) In section 54 of that Act (requirements as to medical evidence), after the words "38(1)" there shall be inserted the words "45A(2)".

(7) In subsection (2) of section 61 of that Act (review of treatment)—

(a) after the words "restriction order" there shall be inserted the words ", limitation direction"; and

(b) in paragraph (b), after the words "section 41(6)" there shall be inserted the words ", 45B(3)".

(8) In subsection (2)(b) of section 69 of that Act (applications to tribunals concerning patients subject to hospital and guardianship orders), after the word "section" there shall be inserted "45B(2),".

(9) In section 70(a) of that Act (applications to tribunals concerning restricted patients), after the words "hospital order" there shall be inserted the words ", hospital direction".

(10) In subsection (1) of section 74 of that Act (restricted patients), after the words "who is subject to" there shall be inserted the words "a limitation direction or".

(11) In subsection (5) of that section, after the word "above" there shall be inserted the words "the relevant hospital direction and the limitation direction or, as the case may be,".

(12) In subsection (6) of that section, after the words "references to", in the second place where they occur, there shall be inserted the words "the hospital direction and the limitation direction or, as the case may be, to".

(13) In section 75(1)(b) of that Act (applications and references concerning conditionally discharged restricted patients), after the words "hospital order" there shall be inserted the words ", hospital direction".

(14) In subsection (1) of section 79 of that Act (interpretation of Part V), after the words "restriction order" there shall be inserted the words ", limitation direction".

(15) In subsection (2) of that section—

(a) after the words "'the relevant hospital order'" there shall be inserted the words ", 'the relevant hospital direction'"; and

(b) after the words "the hospital order" there shall be inserted the words ", the hospital direction".

(16) After subsection (3) of section 92 of that Act (interpretation of Part VI) there shall be inserted the following subsections—

"(4) Sections 80 to 85A above shall have effect as if—

(a) any hospital direction under section 45A above were a transfer direction under section 47 above; and

(b) any limitation direction under section 45A above were a restriction direction under section 49 above.

(5) Sections 80(5), 81(6) and 85(4) above shall have effect as if any reference to a transfer direction given while a patient was serving a sentence of imprisonment imposed by a court included a reference to a hospital direction given by a court after imposing a sentence of imprisonment on a patient."

(17) In subsection (1) of section 117 of that Act (after-care), after the words "transferred to a hospital in pursuance of" there shall be inserted the words "a hospital direction made under section 45A above or".

(18) In subsection (3) of section 143 of that Act (general provisions as to regulations, orders and rules), after the word "section" there shall be inserted the word "45A(10),".

(19) In subsection (1) of section 145 of that Act (interpretation)—

(a) after the definition of "hospital" there shall be inserted the following definition—

"'hospital direction' has the meaning given in section 45A(3)(a) above;";

(b) after the definition of 'interim hospital order' there shall be inserted the following definition—

"'limitation direction' has the meaning given in section 45A(3)(b) above;".

Criminal Justice Act 1988 (c.33)

13. At the end of subsection (2) of section 36 of the Criminal Justice Act 1988 (review of sentencing) there shall be inserted the words "or failed to impose a sentence required by section 2(2), 3(2) or 4(2) of the Crime (Sentences) Act 1997".

Prevention of Terrorism (Temporary Provisions) Act 1989 (c.4)

14. In sub-paragraph (5) of paragraph 9 of Schedule 2 to the Prevention of Terrorism (Temporary Provisions) Act 1989 (exemption from exclusion orders), for the words "section 67 of the Criminal Justice Act 1967" there shall be substituted the words "section 9 of the Crime (Sentences) Act 1997".

Criminal Justice Act 1991 (c.53)

15.—(1) In subsection (1) of section 1 of the 1991 Act (restrictions on imposing custodial sentences), after the words "fixed by law" there shall be inserted the words "or falling to be imposed under section 2(2), 3(2) or 4(2) of the Crime (Sentences) Act 1997".

(2) For subsection (3) of that section there shall be substituted the following subsection—

"(3) Nothing in subsection (2) above shall prevent the court from passing a custodial sentence on the offender if he fails to express his willingness to comply with a requirement which is proposed by the court to be included in a probation order or supervision order and which requires an expression of such willingness."

(3) In subsection (1) of section 2 of that Act (length of custodial sentences), after the words "fixed by law" there shall be inserted the words "or falling to be imposed under section 2(2) of the Crime (Sentences) Act 1997".

(4) At the beginning of subsection (2) of that section there shall be inserted the words "Subject to sections 3(2) and 4(2) of that Act,".

(5) After subsection (4) of that section there shall be inserted the following subsection—

"(5) Subsection (3) above shall not apply in any case where the court passes a custodial sentence falling to be imposed under subsection (2) of section 3 or 4 of the Crime (Sentences) Act 1997 which is for the minimum term specified in that subsection."

(6) In subsection (1) of section 4 of that Act (additional requirements in the case of mentally disordered offenders)—

(a) the words "section 3(1) above applies and" shall cease to have effect; and

(b) after the words "fixed by law" there shall be inserted the words "or falling to be imposed under section 2(2) of the Crime (Sentences) Act 1997".

(7) In subsection (3) of that section, after the words "fixed by law" there shall be inserted the words "or falling to be imposed under section 2(2) of the Crime (Sentences) Act 1997".

(8) In subsection (1) of section 11 of that Act (orders combining probation and community service), after the words "is fixed by law" there shall be inserted the words "or falls to be imposed under section 2(2), 3(2) or 4(2) of the Crime (Sentences) Act 1997".

(9) In subsection (1) of section 12 of that Act (curfew orders), after the words "is fixed by law" there shall be inserted the words "or falls to be imposed under section 2(2), 3(2) or 4(2) of the Crime (Sentences) Act 1997".

(10) In section 32 of that Act (the Parole Board)—

(a) in subsection (1), for the words from "be constituted" to the end there shall be substituted the following paragraphs—

"(a) be constituted in accordance with this Part; and

(b) have the functions conferred by Part II of the Crime (Sentences) Act 1997 ("Part II")."; and

(b) in subsections (3), (4) and (6), for the words "this Part" there shall be substituted the words "Part II".

(11) In sub-paragraph (2) of each of paragraphs 3 and 4 of Schedule 2 to that Act (powers of magistrates' court and Crown Court), for paragraph (b) there shall be substituted the following paragraph—

"(b) in the case of an offender who has wilfully and persistently failed to comply with those requirements, may impose a custodial sentence notwithstanding anything in section 1(2) of this Act."

(12) In sub-paragraph (2)(a)(ii) of paragraph 13 of that Schedule (amendment of requirements of probation or curfew order), after the word "unless" there shall be inserted the words "the offender has expressed his willingness to comply with such a requirement and".

(13) In sub-paragraph (2)(b) of paragraph 14 of that Schedule (amendment of certain requirements of probation order), the words from "being treatment" to the end shall cease to have effect.

Prisoners and Criminal Proceedings (Scotland) Act 1993 (c.9)

16.—(1) In section 10(4) of the Prisoners and Criminal Proceedings (Scotland) Act 1993 (meaning of transferred life prisoner), for the words "section 26 of the Criminal Justice Act 1961" there shall be substituted the words "paragraph 1 of Schedule 1 to the Crime (Sentences) Act 1997".

(2) In Schedule 6 to that Act, in paragraph 1, in the definition of "new provisions", after the word "Act" where it last occurs, there shall be inserted the words "and the Repatriation of Prisoners Act 1984 as it has effect by virtue of paragraphs 6 and 7 of Schedule 2 to the Crime (Sentences) Act 1997".

Criminal Justice and Public Order Act 1994 (c.33)

17. After subsection (2) of section 48 of the Criminal Justice and Public Order Act 1994 (reduction in sentences for guilty pleas) there shall be inserted the following subsection—

"(3) In the case of an offence the sentence for which falls to be imposed under subsection (2) of section 3 or 4 of the Crime (Sentences) Act 1997, nothing in that subsection shall prevent the court, after taking into account any matter referred to in subsection (1) above, from imposing any sentence which is not less than 80 per cent of that specified in that subsection."

Section 56(1).

SCHEDULE 5

TRANSITIONAL PROVISIONS AND SAVINGS

Sentences for offences committed before the commencement of Chapter I of Part II

1. Notwithstanding their repeal by this Act, sections 33, 35 to 47, 49 to 51 and 65 of the 1991 Act shall, so far as applicable and subject to the following provisions of this Schedule, continue to have effect in relation to persons sentenced to determinate sentences of imprisonment for offences committed before the commencement of Chapter I of Part II of this Act.

Consecutive sentences for offences committed before and after that commencement

2.—(1) This paragraph applies where consecutive terms of imprisonment include—

(a) the term of a sentence imposed on an offender for an offence committed after the commencement of Chapter I of Part II of this Act; and

(b) the term of a sentence imposed on him for an offence committed before that commencement.

(2) Subject to sub-paragraphs (3) and (4) below, the time to be served by the offender shall be determined separately in respect of each sentence under whichever of Chapter I of Part II of this Act and Part II of the 1991 Act is applicable to that sentence.

(3) Where the offender was remanded in custody in connection with—

(a) an offence falling within sub-paragraph (1)(a) above; and

(b) an offence falling within sub-paragraph (1)(b) above,

any additional days which have been both conditionally and provisionally awarded to him shall be taken into account for the purposes of Chapter I of Part II of this Act and not for the purposes of Part II of the 1991 Act.

(4) The time to be served by the offender in respect of a sentence falling within sub-paragraph (1)(b) above which—

(a) is for a term of four years or more; and

(b) is not the final sentence,

shall be determined as if section 35(1) of the 1991 Act were omitted.

(5) The offender shall be released when he has served the time required to be served in respect of the final sentence.

(6) Subject to sub-paragraph (7) below, whichever of Chapter I of Part II of this Act and Part II of the 1991 Act is applicable to the final sentence shall apply in relation to the offender after his release.

(7) Notwithstanding anything in Part II of the 1991 Act, the offender's supervision shall be for the period which would be applicable if each of his terms of imprisonment had been imposed in respect of offences committed after the commencement of Chapter I of Part II of this Act.

(8) In this paragraph "the final sentence", in relation to any time, means the sentence which at that time falls to be served after the other or others.

(9) In this paragraph and paragraph 3 below—

"conditionally awarded" means conditionally awarded under prison rules made by virtue of section 42(1) of the 1991 Act;

"provisionally awarded" means provisionally awarded under prison rules having effect by virtue of section 15(2) of this Act;

and any reference to Part II of the 1991 Act includes, unless the context otherwise requires, a reference to section 65 of that Act.

Concurrent sentences for offences committed before and after that commencement

3.—(1) This paragraph applies where terms of imprisonment which are wholly or partly concurrent include—

(a) the term of a sentence imposed on an offender for an offence committed after the commencement of Chapter I of Part II of this Act; and

(b) the term of a sentence imposed on him for an offence committed before that commencement.

(2) Subject to sub-paragraph (3) below, the time to be served by the offender in respect of the final sentence shall be determined under whichever of Chapter I of Part II of this Act and Part II of the 1991 Act is applicable to that sentence.

(3) Where the offender was remanded in custody in connection with—

(a) an offence falling within sub-paragraph (1)(a) above; and

(b) an offence falling within sub-paragraph (1)(b) above,

any additional days which have been both conditionally and provisionally awarded to him shall be taken into account only for the purposes of whichever of Chapter I of Part II of this Act and Part II of the 1991 Act is applicable to the final sentence.

(4) The offender shall be released when he has served the time required to be served in respect of the final sentence.

SCH. 5

(5) Subject to sub-paragraph (6) below, whichever of Chapter I of Part II of this Act and Part II of the 1991 Act is applicable to the final sentence shall apply in relation to the offender after his release.

(6) Notwithstanding anything in Part II of the 1991 Act, the offender's supervision shall be for the period which would be applicable if each of his terms of imprisonment had been imposed in respect of offences committed after the commencement of Chapter I of Part II of this Act.

(7) Where at any time a sentence falling within sub-paragraph (1)(a) above ("sentence A") becomes the final sentence in place of a sentence falling within sub-paragraph (1)(b) above ("sentence B") either—

> (a) because the term of sentence A is increased on appeal; or

> (b) because sentence B is set aside, or its term is reduced, on appeal,

then, for each assessment period for the purposes of section 11 of this Act beginning before that time, the prescribed person or, as the case may be, the Secretary of State shall assume, for the purposes of subsection (2) or (3) of that section, that the prisoner's behaviour was such as to entitle him to the maximum number of early release days available under that subsection.

(8) In this paragraph "the final sentence", in relation to any time, means the sentence which at that time will have the later or latest release date on the following assumptions, namely—

> (a) that the time to be served in respect of a sentence falling within sub-paragraph (1)(a) above is equal to the term imposed by the court less the number of days (if any) directed by the court to count as time served as part of the sentence; and

> (b) that the time to be served in respect of a sentence falling within sub-paragraph (1)(b) above is equal to the appropriate proportion of the term imposed by the court less any period by which the sentence falls to be reduced under section 67 of the Criminal Justice Act 1967.

1967 c.80.

(9) In sub-paragraph (8) above "the appropriate proportion" means one-half in the case of a term of less than four years and two thirds in the case of a term of four years or more.

Crediting of periods of remand in custody

4. In relation to any time between the commencement of section 9 of this Act and the commencement of Chapter I of Part II of this Act, sections 34, 41 and 47 of the 1991 Act shall have effect as if any reference (however expressed) to a relevant period by which a sentence falls to be reduced under section 67 of the 1967 Act were a reference to a number of days directed under section 9 of this Act to count as time served as part of a sentence.

Duty to release certain life prisoners

5.—(1) In relation to any time before the commencement of section 9 of this Act, section 28 of this Act shall have effect as if, in paragraph (b) of subsection (3), for the words "of any direction it would have given under section 9 above" there were substituted the words "which section 67 of the Criminal Justice Act 1967 would have had".

(2) In relation to any time before the commencement of Chapter I of Part II of this Act, section 28 of this Act shall have effect as if—

> (a) after paragraph (b) of subsection (3), there were inserted the words "and

>> "(c) the provisions of this section as compared with those of sections 33(2) and 35(1) of the 1991 Act"; and

> (b) in paragraph (c) of subsection (7), for the words from "the time when" to the end there were substituted the words "he has served one-half of that sentence".

(3) Section 28(7) of this Act shall have effect as if—

    (a) any reference of a prisoner's case made to the Parole Board under section 32(2) or 34(4) of the 1991 Act had been made under section 28(6) of this Act; and

    (b) any such reference made under section 39(4) of that Act had been made under section 32(4) of this Act.

Life prisoners transferred to England and Wales

6. In relation to any time before the commencement of Schedule 1 to this Act, section 33 of this Act shall have effect as if, in paragraph (b)(i) of subsection (4), for the words "paragraph 1 of Schedule 1 to this Act" there were substituted the words "section 26 of the Criminal Justice Act 1961".

1961 c.39.

Recall of life prisoners while on licence

7.—(1) Section 32(3) and (4) of this Act shall have effect as if any life prisoner recalled to prison under subsection (1) or (2) of section 39 of the 1991 Act had been recalled to prison under the corresponding subsection of section 32 of this Act.

(2) Section 32(4) of this Act shall have effect as if any representations made by a life prisoner under section 39(3) of the 1991 Act had been made under section 32(3) of this Act.

Transfers of prisoners: general

8. In relation to any person serving a determinate custodial sentence in respect of an offence committed before the commencement of Chapter I of Part II of this Act, paragraph 6 of Schedule 1 to this Act shall have effect as if, in sub-paragraph (3)(b) of that paragraph, for the words "recalled to prison under the licence" there were substituted the words "recalled or returned to prison".

Transfers of prisoners from England and Wales to Scotland

9.—(1) In relation to any person serving a determinate custodial sentence imposed in respect of an offence committed before the commencement of Chapter I of Part II of this Act, paragraph 8 of Schedule 1 to this Act shall have effect as if—

    (a) references in sub-paragraph (2) to provisions of that Chapter were references to sections 33, 35 to 39, 41 to 46 and 65 of the 1991 Act and paragraphs 8, 10 to 13 and 19 of Schedule 12 to that Act, so far as relating to short-term or long-term prisoners;

    (b) references in sub-paragraph (4) to provisions of that Chapter were references to sections 37 to 39, 43 to 46 and 65 of the 1991 Act and paragraphs 8, 10 to 13 and 19 of Schedule 12 to that Act, so far as so relating;

    (c) the reference in sub-paragraph (5) to any provision of Part II of this Act were a reference to any provision of Part II of that Act; and

    (d) section 67 of the Criminal Justice Act 1967 (computation of sentences of imprisonment passed in England and Wales) or, as the case may require, section 9 of this Act extended to Scotland.

1967 c.80.

(2) In relation to any time before the commencement of Chapter II of Part II of this Act, paragraph 8 of Schedule 1 to this Act shall have effect as if—

    (a) references in sub-paragraph (2) to provisions of that Chapter were references to sections 34 to 37, 39, 43 and 46 of the 1991 Act and paragraphs 8 and 9 of Schedule 12 to that Act, so far as relating to life prisoners;

(b) references in sub-paragraph (4) to provisions of that Chapter were references to sections 37, 39, 43 and 46 of the 1991 Act and paragraphs 8 and 9 of Schedule 12 to that Act, so far as so relating; and

(c) the reference in sub-paragraph (5) to any provision of Part II of this Act were a reference to any provision of Part II of that Act.

Transfers of prisoners from England and Wales to Northern Ireland

10.—(1) In relation to any person serving a determinate custodial sentence imposed in respect of an offence committed before the commencement of Chapter I of Part II of this Act, paragraph 9 of Schedule 1 to this Act shall have effect as if—

(a) in sub-paragraph (1), paragraph (a) and, in paragraph (b), the words "to that and" were omitted;

(b) references in sub-paragraph (2) to provisions of that Chapter were references to sections 33, 35 to 46 and 65 of the 1991 Act and paragraphs 8, 10 to 13 and 19 of Schedule 12 to that Act, so far as relating to short-term or long-term prisoners;

(c) references in sub-paragraph (4) to provisions of that Chapter were references to sections 37 to 40, 43 to 46 and 65 of the 1991 Act and paragraphs 8, 10 to 13 and 19 of Schedule 12 to that Act, so far as so relating;

(d) the reference in sub-paragraph (6) to any provision of Part II of this Act were a reference to any provision of Part II of that Act; and

(e) section 67 of the Criminal Justice Act 1967 or, as the case may require, section 9 of this Act extended to Northern Ireland.

(2) In relation to any time before the commencement of Chapter II of Part II of this Act, paragraph 9 of Schedule 1 to this Act shall have effect as if—

(a) references in sub-paragraph (2) to provisions of that Chapter were references to sections 34 to 37, 39, 43 and 46 of the 1991 Act and paragraphs 8 and 9 of Schedule 12 to that Act, so far as relating to life prisoners;

(b) references in sub-paragraph (4) to provisions of that Chapter were references to sections 37, 39, 43 and 46 of the 1991 Act and paragraphs 8 and 9 of Schedule 12 to that Act, so far as so relating; and

(c) the reference in sub-paragraph (5) to any provision of Part II of this Act were a reference to any provision of Part II of that Act.

Transfers of prisoners from Scotland to England and Wales

11.—(1) In relation to any prisoner sentenced on or after 1st October 1993 in respect of an offence committed before the commencement of section 33 of the Crime and Punishment (Scotland) Act 1997 ("the 1997 Act"), paragraph 10 of Schedule 1 to this Act shall have effect as if—

(a) references in sub-paragraph (2) to sections 15, 18 and 19 of the Prisoners and Criminal Proceedings (Scotland) Act 1993 ("the 1993 Act") and to sections 33(5), 34, 37 and 39 of the 1997 Act were references to sections 1 to 3, 5, 6(1)(a) and (b)(i) and (iii), 9, 11 to 13, 15 to 21 and 27 of, and Schedules 2 and 6 to, the 1993 Act;

(b) references in sub-paragraph (5) to sections 15, 18 and 19 of the 1993 Act and to sections 33(5) and 37 of the 1997 Act were references to sections 11 to 13, 15 to 21 and 27 of, and Schedules 2 and 6 to, the 1993 Act;

(c) references in that sub-paragraph to sections 2(4), 11 to 13 and 17 of the 1993 Act were references to sections 26 and 28 of the Prisons (Scotland) Act 1989 ("the 1989 Act"); and

(d) the reference in sub-paragraph (7) to any provision of Part I of the 1993 Act or Part III of the 1997 Act were a reference to any provision of the 1993 Act.

(2) In relation to any prisoner to whom the existing provisions apply, paragraph 10 of Schedule 1 to this Act shall have effect as if—

(a) references in sub-paragraph (2) to sections 15, 18 and 19 of the 1993 Act and to sections 33(5), 34, 37 and 39 of the 1997 Act were references to Schedule 6 to the 1993 Act and to the following existing provisions, namely, sections 18, 19(4), 22, 24, 26, 28 to 30, 32 and 43 of, and Schedule 1 to, the 1989 Act and any rules made under section 18 or 39 of that Act;

(b) references in sub-paragraph (5) to sections 15, 18 and 19 of the 1993 Act and to sections 33(5) and 37 of the 1997 Act were references to the said Schedule 6 and to the following existing provisions, namely, sections 30, 32 and 43 of the 1989 Act; and

(c) the reference in sub-paragraph (7) to any provision of Part I of the 1993 Act or Part III of the 1997 Act were a reference to any provision of the said Schedule 6 or the 1989 Act.

(3) In sub-paragraph (1) above the reference to section 6(1)(b)(i) of the 1993 Act is a reference to that provision so far as it relates to a person sentenced under section 205(3) of the Criminal Procedure (Scotland) Act 1995; and in sub-paragraph (2) above— 1995 c.46.

(a) the reference to section 19(4) of the 1989 Act is a reference to that provision so far as it applies section 24 of that Act in relation to persons detained in young offenders institutions; and

(b) any reference to the existing provisions is a reference to the existing provisions within the meaning of Schedule 6 to the 1993 Act.

Transfers of prisoners from Scotland to Northern Ireland

12.—(1) In relation to any prisoner sentenced on or after 1st October 1993 for an offence committed before the commencement of section 33 of the Crime and Punishment (Scotland) Act 1997 ("the 1997 Act"), paragraph 11 of Schedule 1 to this Act shall have effect as if— 1997 c.48

(a) references in sub-paragraph (2) to sections 15, 18 and 19 of the Prisoners and Criminal Proceedings (Scotland) Act 1993 ("the 1993 Act") and sections 33(5), 34, 37 and 39 of the 1997 Act were references to sections 1, 2, 3, 5, 6(1)(a) and (b)(i) and (iii), 9, 11 to 13, 15 to 21 and 27 of, and Schedules 2 and 6 to, the 1993 Act; 1993 c.9.

(b) references in sub-paragraph (4) to sections 15, 18 and 19 of the 1993 Act and to sections 33(5) and 37 of the 1997 Act were references to sections 11 to 13, 15 to 21 and 27 of, and Schedules 2 and 6 to, the 1993 Act;

(c) references in that sub-paragraph to sections 2(4), 11 to 13 and 17 of the 1993 Act were references to sections 26 and 28 of the Prisons (Scotland) Act 1989 ("the 1989 Act"); and 1989 c.45.

(d) the reference in sub-paragraph (5) to any provision of Part I of the 1993 Act or Part III of the 1997 Act were a reference to any provision of the 1993 Act, and the Table set out in that sub-paragraph contained the following entry—

"Probation officer appointed for or assigned to such petty sessions area   Probation Officer appointed by the Probation Board for Northern Ireland"

(2) In relation to any prisoner to whom the existing provisions apply, paragraph 11 of Schedule 1 to this Act shall have effect as if—

(a) references in sub-paragraph (2) to sections 15, 18 and 19 of the 1993 Act and to sections 33(5), 34, 37 and 39 of the 1997 Act were references to Schedule 6 to the 1993 Act and to the following existing provisions, namely, sections 18, 19(4), 22, 24, 26, 28 to 30, 32 and 43, and Schedule 1 to, the 1989 Act and any rules made under section 18 or 39 of that Act;

(b) references in sub-paragraph (4) to sections 15, 18 and 19 of the 1993 Act and sections 33(5) and 37 of the 1997 Act were references to the said Schedule 6 and to the following existing provisions, namely, sections 30, 32 and 43 of the 1989 Act; and

(c) the reference in sub-paragraph (6) to any provision of Part I of the 1993 Act or Part III of the 1997 Act were a reference to any provision of the said Schedule 6 or the 1989 Act.

(3) Sub-paragraph (3) of paragraph 11 above shall apply for the purposes of this paragraph as it applies for the purposes of that paragraph.

Interpretation

13. In this Schedule—

"life prisoner" has the same meaning as in Chapter II of Part II of this Act;

"term of imprisonment" includes a sentence of detention in a young offender institution or under section 53 of the 1933 Act.

SCHEDULE 6

REPEALS

Section 56(2).

Chapter	Short title	Extent of repeal
9 & 10 Eliz. 2 c.39.	Criminal Justice Act 1961.	Part III. In section 36(1), the words "or under Part III". In section 38, in subsection (3), the words "of Part III and" and, in subsection (6), the words "and of any enactment referred to in Part III of this Act". In section 39, in subsection (1), the definitions of "appropriate institution" and "responsible Minister", and subsection (1A). In section 42, in subsection (1), the words "Part III except section thirty-three" and, in subsection (2), the words "Part III".
1967 c.80.	Criminal Justice Act 1967.	Section 67.
1973 c.62.	Powers of Criminal Courts Act 1973.	In section 2(3), the words from "and the court" to the end. In section 14(2), the words "the offender consents and". In section 42(1), the words "or section 62 of the Criminal Justice Act 1967".
1983 c.20.	Mental Health Act 1983.	In section 37(4), the words "in the event of such an order being made by the court". In section 47(1), the words "(not being a mental nursing home)". In Schedule 1, in Part II, in paragraph 5, the word "and" immediately following sub-paragraph (a).
1991 c.53.	Criminal Justice Act 1991.	In section 4(1), the words "section 3(1) above applies and". In section 12, in subsection (1), the words "of or over the age of sixteen years" and, in subsection (5), the words from "and the court" to the end. Sections 33 to 51. Section 65.

Chapter	Short title	Extent of repeal
1991 c.53—*cont.*	Criminal Justice Act 1991.—*cont.*	In Schedule 2, in paragraph 14, in sub-paragraph (2)(b), the words from "being treatment" to the end.

© Crown copyright 1997

Printed in the UK by The Stationery Office Limited
under the authority and superintendence of Peter Macdonald, Controller of
Her Majesty's Stationery Office and Queen's Printer of Acts of Parliament